Gifted and Talented Workbook
Fifth Grade

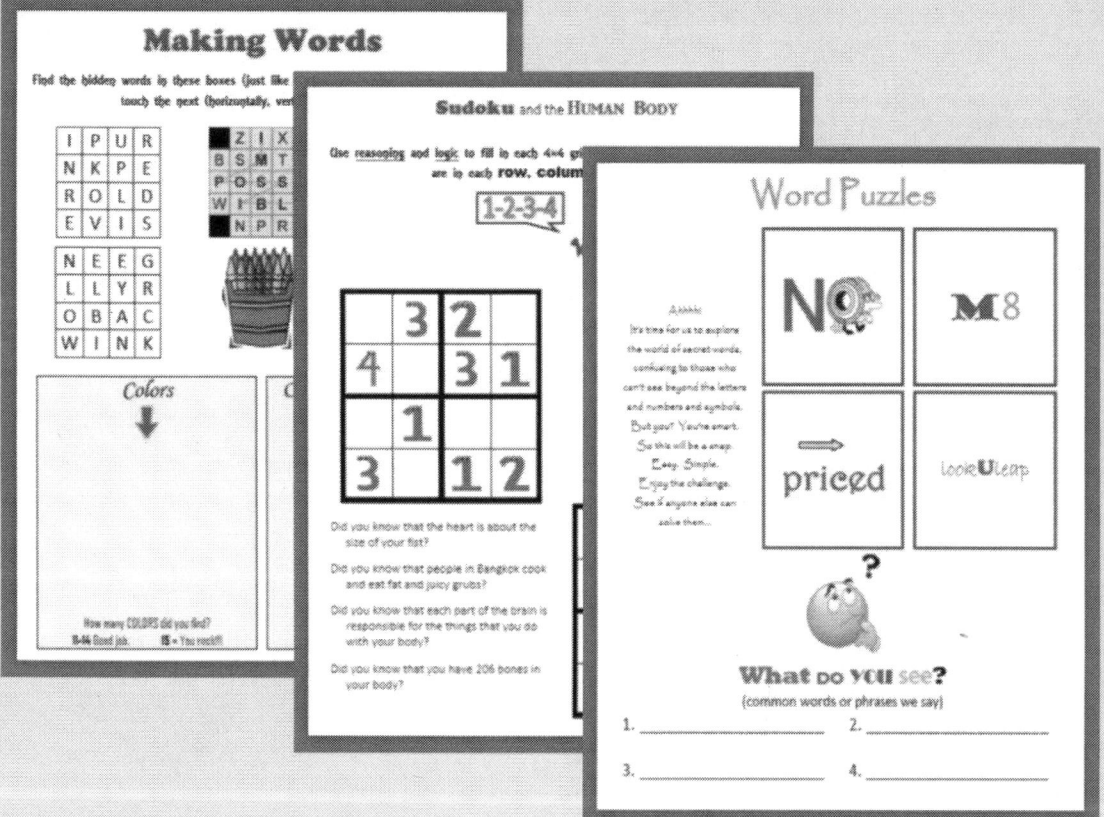

100 Thinking Activities

by C. Mahoney

Life is about choices...

1 – Describe a flower to a blind person.

2 – Anagrams Challenge

Directions: Match the pair of anagrams (use a connecting arrow).

Directions: Write the anagram pairs below:

_____ and _____   _____ and _____   _____ and _____
_____ and _____   _____ and _____   _____ and _____
_____ and _____   _____ and _____   _____ and _____

3 – Different is okay...

Describe four ways that you are <u>different</u> from your brother or sister in what you like and what you don't like.

1. _____

2. _____

3. _____

4. _____

4 – Making Words

Find the hidden words in these boxes (just like Boggle). Each letter in a word must touch the next (horizontally, vertically, or diagonally).

I	P	U	R
N	K	P	E
R	O	L	D
E	V	I	S

	Z	I	X	
B	S	M	T	J
P	O	S	S	V
W	I	B	L	E
	N	P	R	

Y	A	E	G
A	N	R	I
R	G	U	E
O	E	L	B

N	E	E	G
L	L	Y	R
O	B	A	C
W	I	N	K

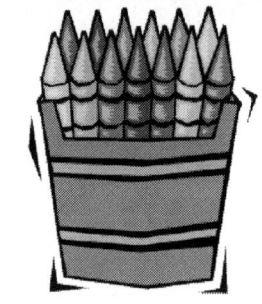

D	H	C	P
L	G	A	E
R	O	H	T
B	W	N	I

Colors

How many COLORS did you find?
11-14 Good job.   **15** = You rock!!!

Other words you found

How many other words did you find?
15-19 Good job.   **20** = You rock!!!

5 – Symmetry

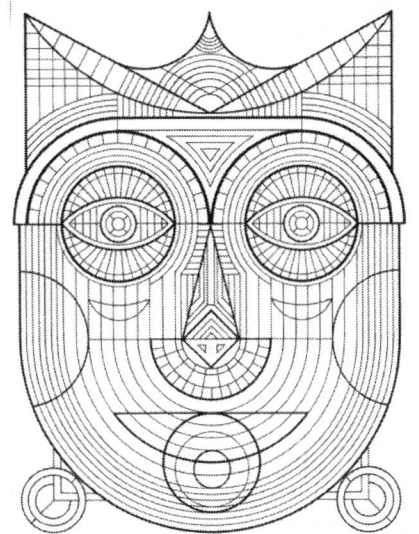

There are __ lines of symmetry.

There are __ lines of symmetry.

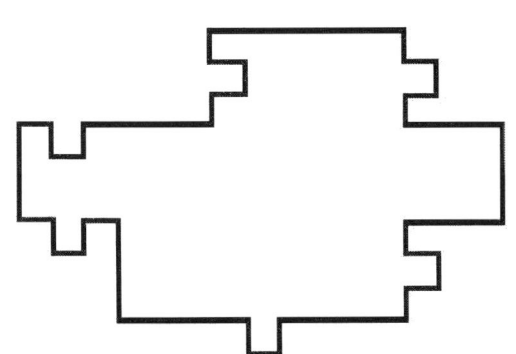

There are __ lines of symmetry.

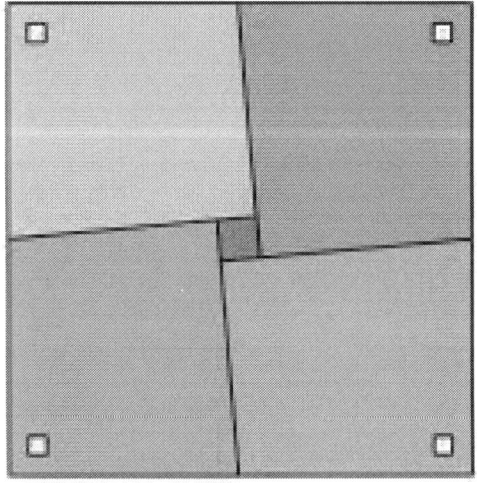

There are __ lines of symmetry.

6 – Word Puzzles

Solve these brainteasers

Hints:

Where is a letter or number located in the frame?

What sound does a letter or number make?

Which direction is a word written?

What is missing?

What object is in the frame?

L + **EV** + 8

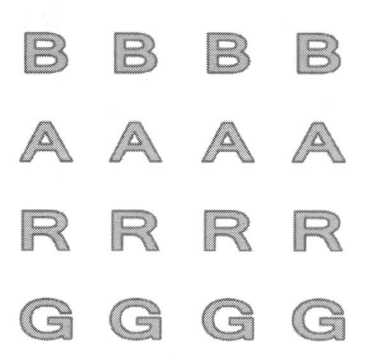

step qəʇsdəʇs

What DO YOU see?
(common words or phrases we say)

1. _____ 2. _____

3. _____ 4. _____

7 – Weather Sudoku

Use reasoning and logic to fill in each 4×4 grid so that each ROW, COLUMN and SQUARE has all four weather symbols.

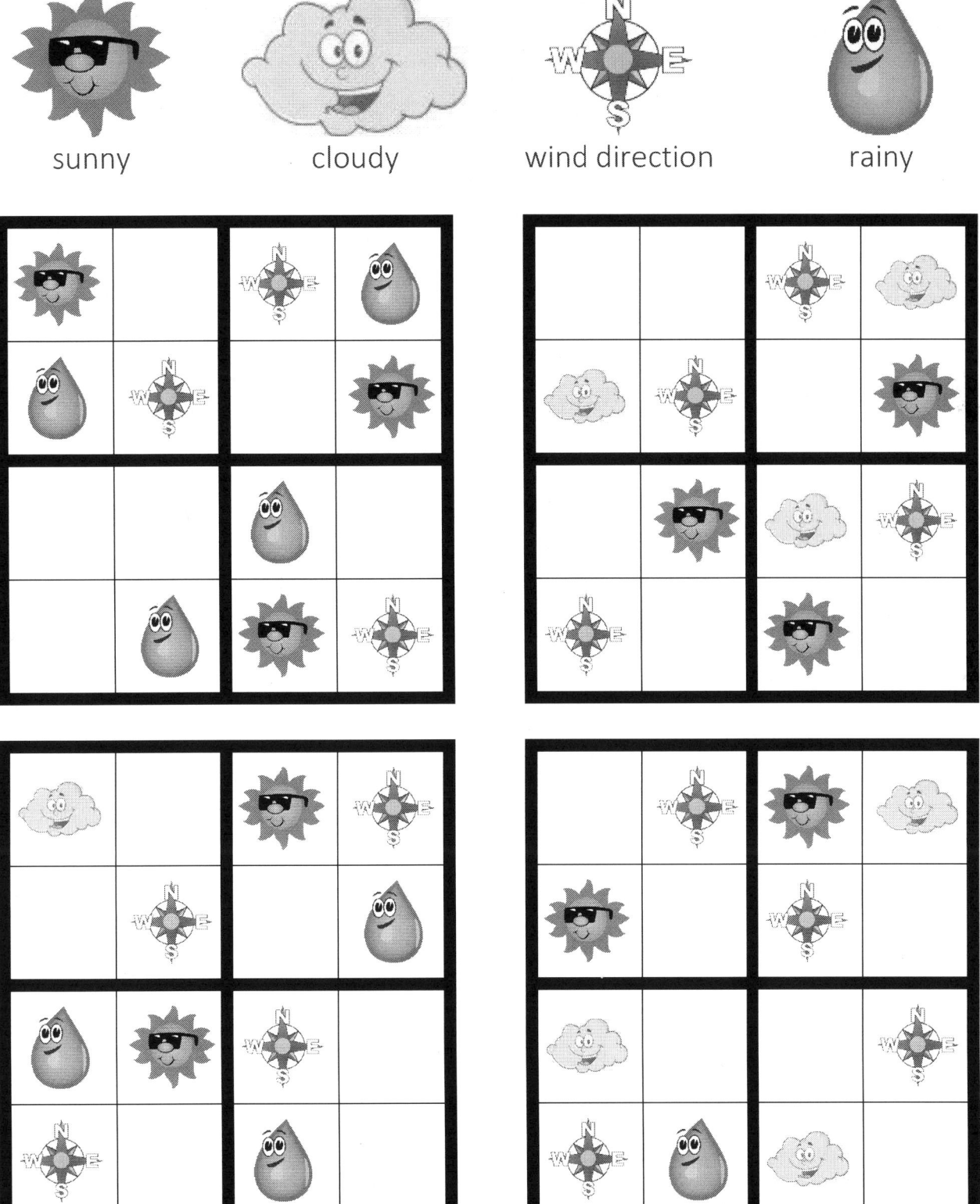

sunny   cloudy   wind direction   rainy

8 – Analyzing What People Say

"Spirituality is not to be learned by flight from the world, or by running away from things, or by turning solitary and going apart from the world. Rather, we must learn an inner solitude wherever or with whomsoever we may be. We must learn to penetrate things and find God there."

- **Meister Eckhart**

My Thoughts and Opinions

_____
_____
_____
_____
_____
_____

9 – Compare and Contrast

What is the **SAME** and what is **DIFFERENT**?

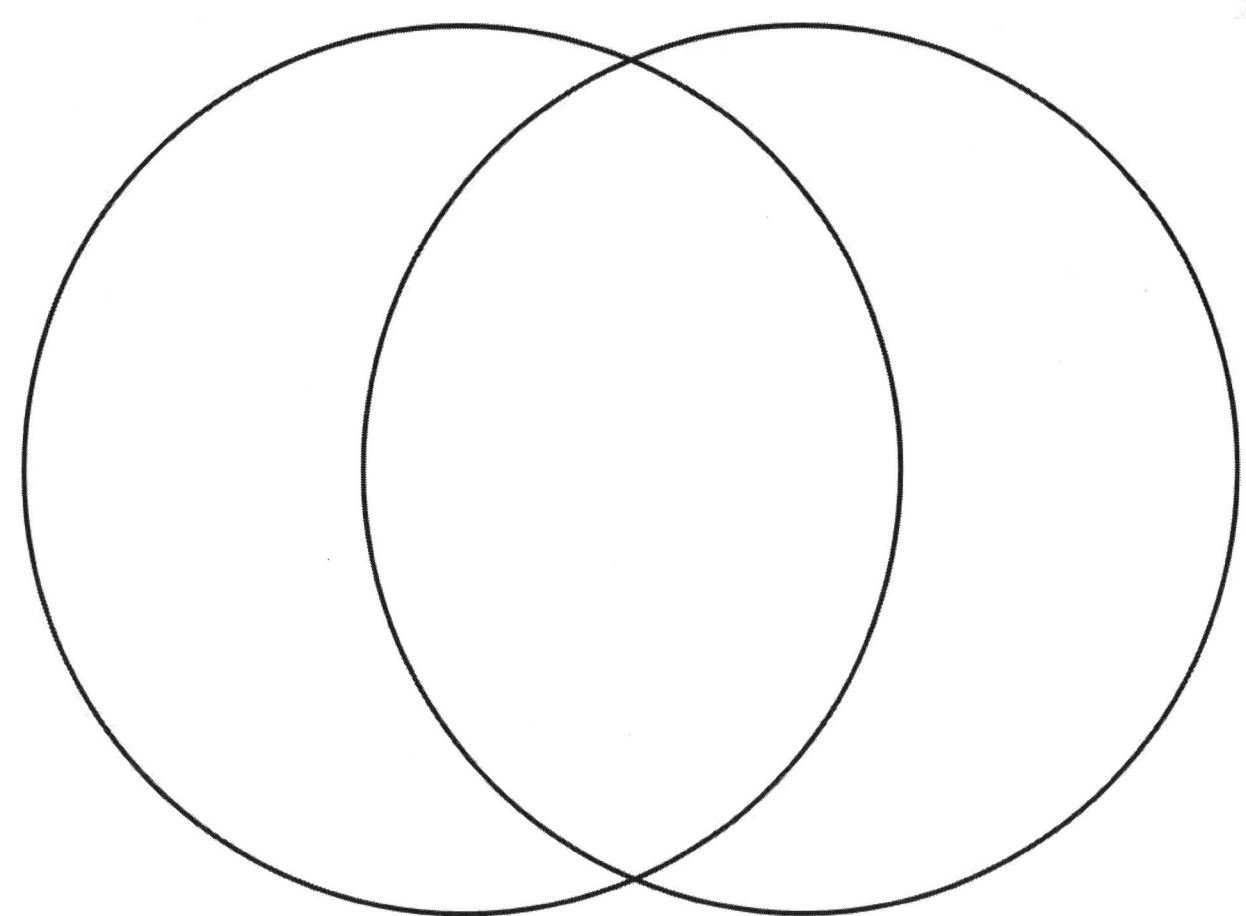

10 – Types of Birds

Birds.
It seems that they are everywhere: in trees, in bushes, on the ground, in the air, and even in this puzzle.
Can you find them?
They can be **horizontal**, **vertical**, **diagonal**, **forwards**, or **backwards**.
Oh, I filled the 13 unused squares with the letter Q.

```
B O O K C U C D R I B K C A L B
L C O O T E G D I R T R A P Q G
U Q Q C R A N E L G A E R L W O
E Q Q M Q U H A W K C U D Q Q L
J R D O R K E E D A K C I H C D
A E R C E Q S T O R K Q N Q H F
Y H I K K E W R E N E V A R I I
T C B I C R A N I B O R L E C N
N T G N E U N A C I L E P E K C
A A N G P T P I G E O N Q H E H
R C I B D L L L U G A E S W N N
O T M I O U S P A R R O W O W R
M A M R O V E S U O M T I T O E
R N U D W R O A D R U N N E R T
O G H K I N G F I S H E R Q C T
C F L Y C A T C H E R E V O D I
A L B A T R O S S R O D N O C B
```

Find these types of birds

albatross, auk, bittern, blackbird, blue jay, cardinal, chickadee, chicken, condor, coot, cormorant, crane, crow, cuckoo, dove, duck, eagle, flycatcher, gnatcatcher, goldfinch, hawk, hummingbird, kingfisher, mockingbird, owl, partridge, pelican, pigeon, raven, roadrunner, robin, seagull, sparrow, stork, swan, titmouse, towhee, vulture, woodpecker, wren

11 – Using Your Imagination

A boy gets ready to throw the snowball at the new kid, but when he turns around, the kid is a monster. What do they say to each other?

12 – Who do you love the most?

13 – Synonyms for the letter A

Directions: Match the pairs of synonyms with the scrambled words on the right. The first is done for you.

abandon = desert
abdomen = _____
above = _____
absurd = _____
ache = _____
acquire = _____
adore = _____
alien = _____
alike = _____
allegiance = _____
allow = _____
amuse = _____
angry = _____
annoy = _____
answer = _____

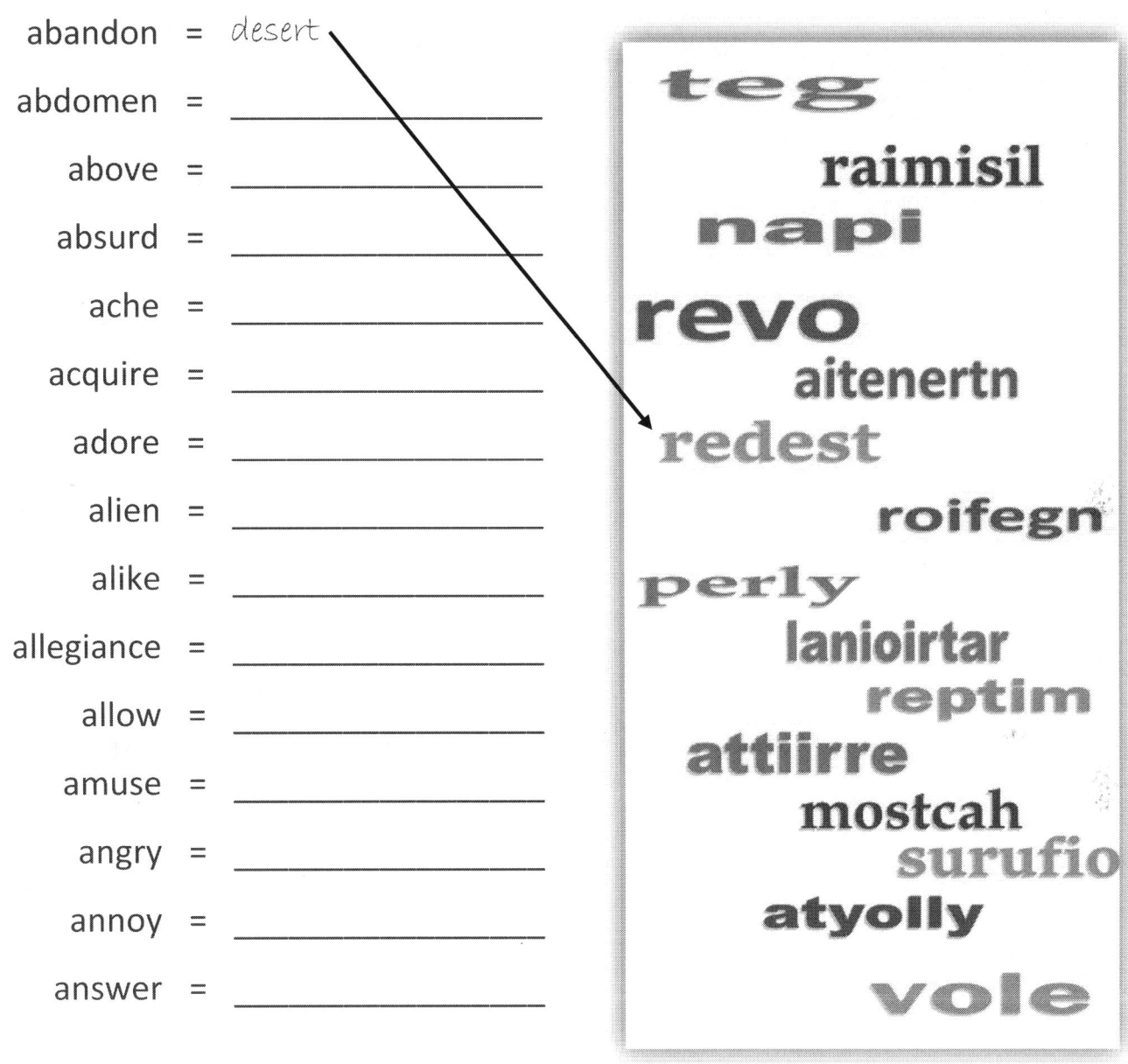

teg
raimisil
napi
revo
aitenertn
redest
roifegn
perly
lanioirtar
reptim
attiirre
mostcah
surufio
atyolly
vole

Directions: Write sentences using A-synonyms, placing two different words in each sentence.

1

2

3

14 – Counting and Comparing Coins

How many **quarters** *are there?* ___
How many **nickels** *are there?* ___
How many **dollars** *are there?* ___
How many more **dimes** are there than **nickels**? ___ - ___ = ___
How many more **nickels** are there than **dollars**? ___ - ___ = ___
How many more **pennies** are there than **nickels**? ___ - ___ = ___
What is the *value* of the **nickels**? $_____
What is the *value* of the **pennies**? $_____
What is the *value* of the **quarters**? $_____
What is the *value* of the **dimes**? $_____
Compare the *value* of the **dimes** to the **nickels**: $____ > $_____
Compare the *value* of the **quarters** to the **dimes**: $____ < $_____
What is the *value* of the **dimes** and **quarters**? $____ + $____ = $____
What is the *value* of the **pennies** and **nickels**? $____ + $____ = $____
What is the total *value* of ALL the coins? $_____

15 – Comparing Shapes

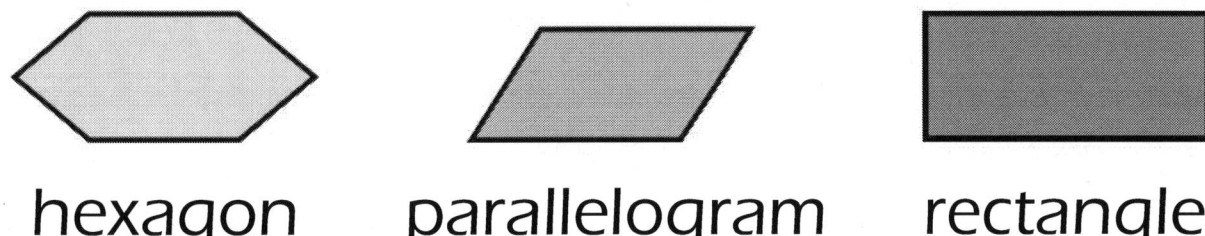

hexagon   parallelogram   rectangle

What is the **same**?

What is **different**?	What is **different**?	What is **different**?
⬇	⬇	⬇

16 – What at home annoys you?

17 – Surroundings

- a squirrel in nearby tree
- a hawk flying overhead
- sun shining from far away
- slight wind blowing grass
- a dragonfly flying above the reeds
- an ant on a floating leaf
- a lizard on a trail just to the right
- insect larvae swimming under water
- a frog jumping onto rock
- MIDDLE OF THE DAY

_____
_____
_____
_____
_____
_____
_____
_____
_____
_____
_____
_____

18 – Spelling Unscramble for Our Earth

Directions: Unscramble the letters to form words related to Earth Day (the picture may give you a clue).

kehoc = _____ gnorist = _____ ractfoy = _____

clertel = _____ nhikt = _____

laytheh = _____ sturangfrit = _____ sceerexi = _____

19 – Making Words

Find the hidden words in these boxes (just like Boggle). Each letter in a word must touch the next (horizontally, vertically, or diagonally).

V	E	L	E
E	N	N	E
T	V	I	R
X	N	H	T

	Z	I	X	
B	S	M	T	J
P	O	S	S	V
W	I	B	L	E
	N	P	R	

G	H	T	W
R	I	E	L
U	N	V	X
O	F	E	I

E	E	N	O
V	T	V	S
X	U	R	E
T	F	O	Z

T	E	E	N
O	R	X	V
W	I	E	I
T	H	S	F

Numbers

Other words you found

How many NUMBERS did you find?
11-14 Good job.   **15** = You rock!!!

How many other words did you find?
15-19 Good job.   **20** = You rock!!!

20 – Symmetry

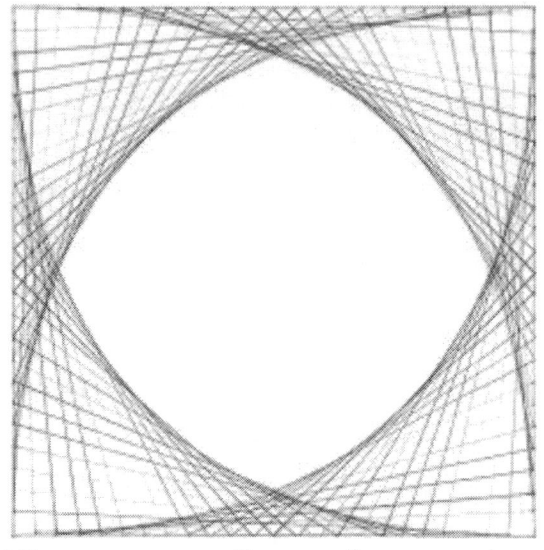

There are __ lines of symmetry.

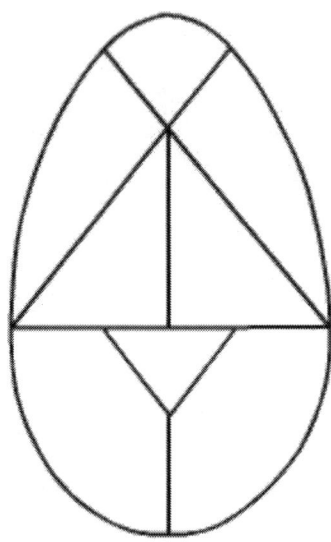

There are __ lines of symmetry.

There are __ lines of symmetry.

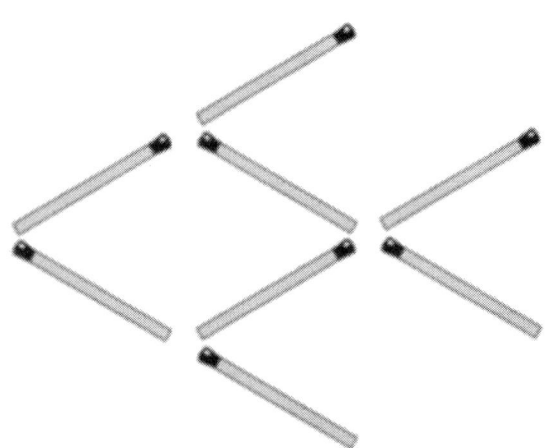

There are __ lines of symmetry.

21 – Word Puzzles

Solve these brainteasers

Hints:
Where is a letter or number located in the frame?

What sound does a letter or number make?

Which direction is a word written?

What is missing?

What object is in the frame?

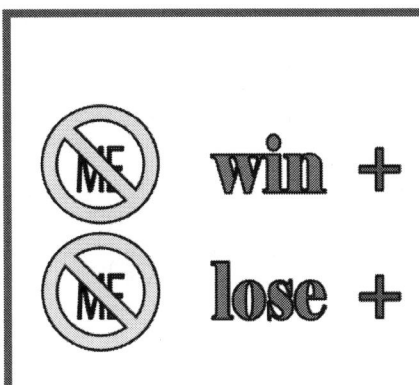

calmSTORM

all **4** zero

actio_

What DO YOU see?
(common words or phrases we say)

1. _____   2. _____

3. _____   4. _____

22 – Sums and Differences

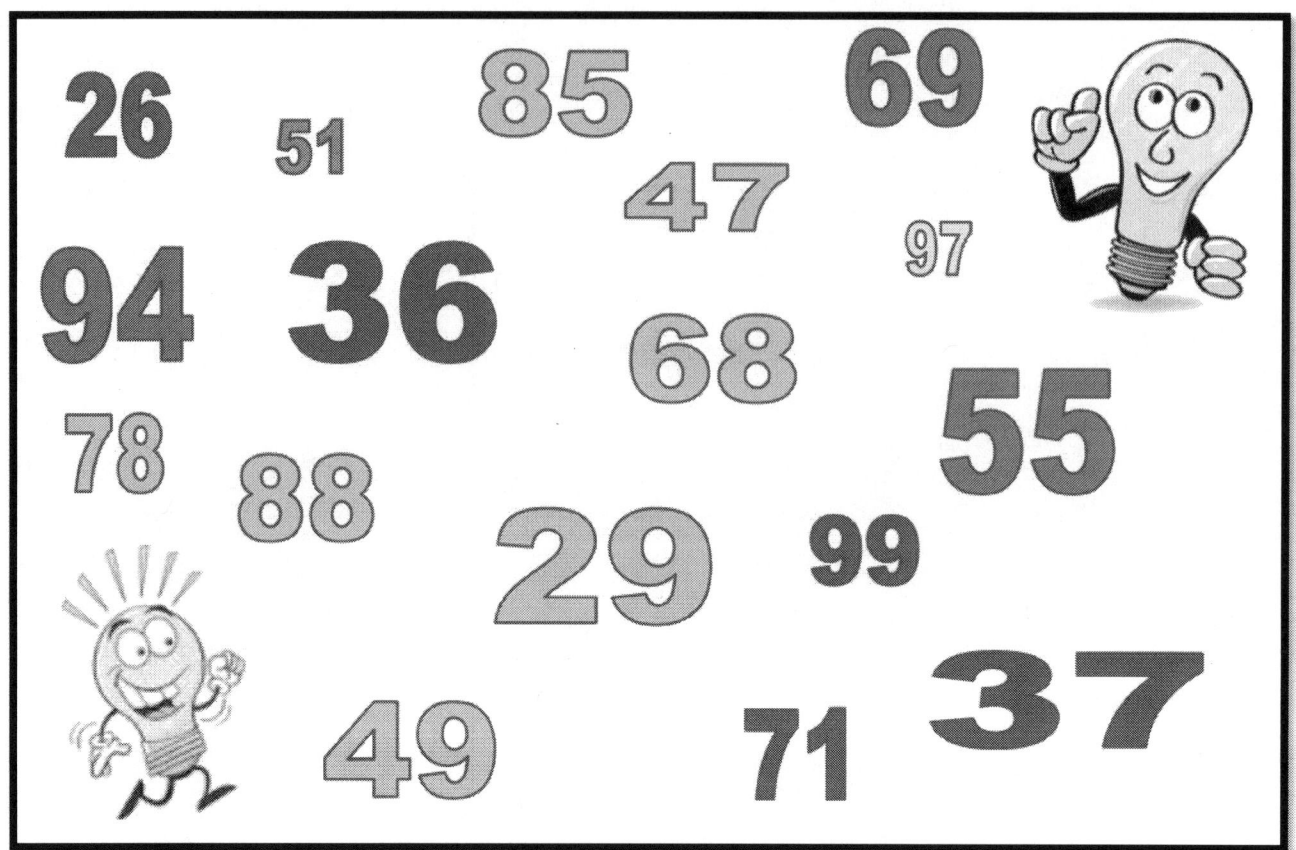

How many numbers are <u>ODD</u>? _____

How many numbers are <u>EVEN</u>? _____

What is the sum of the numbers with a <u>seven</u>? _____

What is the sum of the numbers with an <u>eight</u>? _____

What is the sum of the numbers in their <u>nineties</u>? _____

What is the difference between the <u>largest</u> ODD number and the <u>smallest</u> EVEN number? _____ - _____ = _____

What is the difference between the <u>largest</u> EVEN number and the <u>smallest</u> ODD number? _____ - _____ = _____

23 – How do we use a COIN?

Falkland Islands

24 – Air Travel

Select one of these three stamps to draw below.

Use colored pencils, crayons or markers. Be neat and accurate.

25 – Impossible Conversation

While looking for interesting bugs, a curious boy discovers something new and three-eyed. What do they say to each other?

26 – Where have you been this week?

27 – The Flag of United States of America

Draw the **American Flag**. Use colored pencils, crayons, or markers. Be neat and accurate.

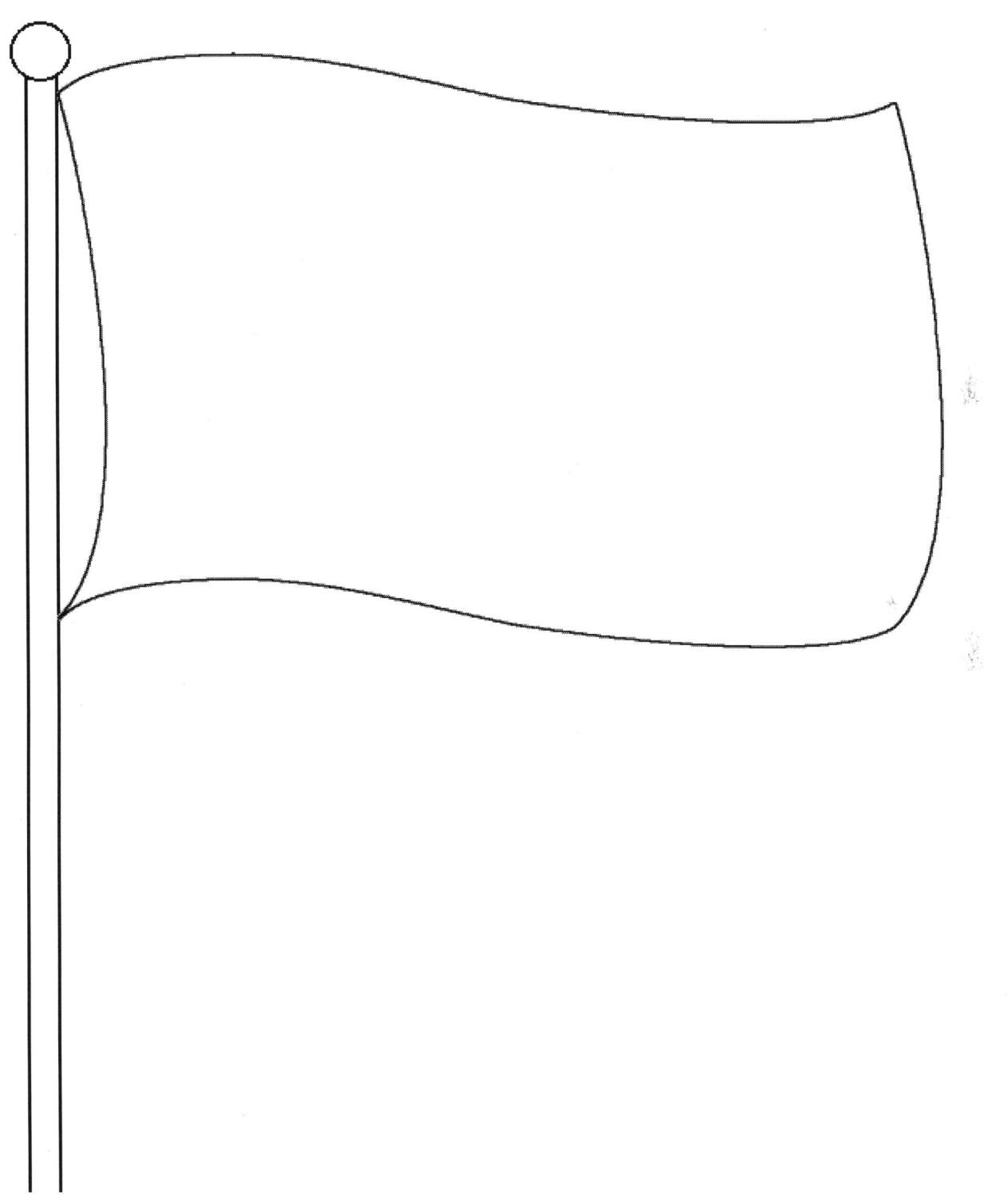

28 – Frankenstein and the Spider

Frankenstein sees a spider playing baseball and asks him a series of questions. What do they say to each other?

29 – Multiplication

9	0	7	6	5	3	2	1	9	0	7	6	4
×4	×4	×4	×4	×4	×4	×4	×4	×4	×4	×4	×4	×4

8	9	6	5	3	2	9	0	7	6	5	1	9
×4	×4	×4	×4	×4	×4	×4	×4	×4	×4	×4	×4	×4

8	5	6	4	3	2	1	0	9	6	7	8	5
×4	×4	×4	×4	×4	×4	×4	×4	×4	×4	×4	×4	×4

9	6	5	3	4	6	9	8	6	5	4	3	2
×4	×4	×4	×4	×4	×4	×4	×4	×4	×4	×4	×4	×4

8	6	4	3	1	2	9	8	6	7	5	3	4
×4	×4	×4	×4	×4	×4	×4	×4	×4	×4	×4	×4	×4

Write the word name and expanded form for each product

standard form	word name	expanded form
4	_____	_____
8	_____	_____
12	_____	_____
16	_____	_____
20	_____	_____
24	_____	_____
28	_____	_____
32	_____	_____
36	_____	_____
40	_____	_____

30 – Seeing Circles

There are ___ circles.

There are ___ circles.

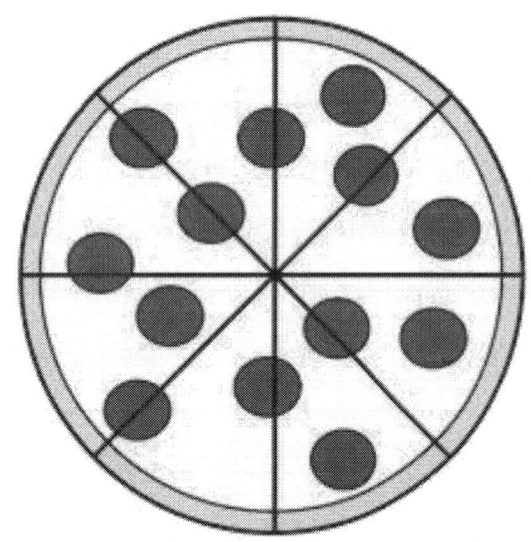

There are ___ circles.

There are ___ circles.

31 – Why do we close doors?

32 – Sudoku and the Human Body

Use reasoning and logic to fill in each 4×4 grid so that the numbers 1, 2, 3 and 4 are in each **row**, **column** and **square**.

	3	2	
4		3	1
	1		
3		1	2

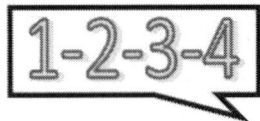

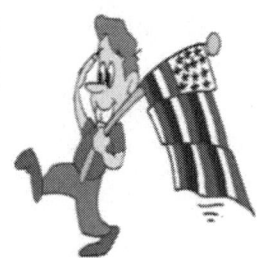

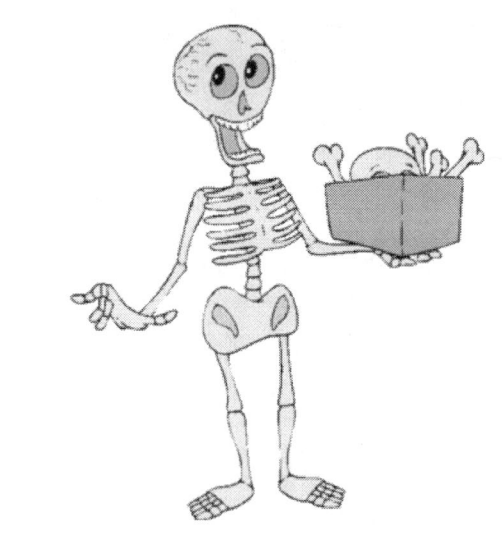

Did you know that the heart is about the size of your fist?

Did you know that people in Bangkok cook and eat fat and juicy grubs?

Did you know that each part of the brain is responsible for the things that you do with your body?

Did you know that you have 206 bones in your body?

		4	
2	4		1
3		1	
	1	2	

33 – What do you see?

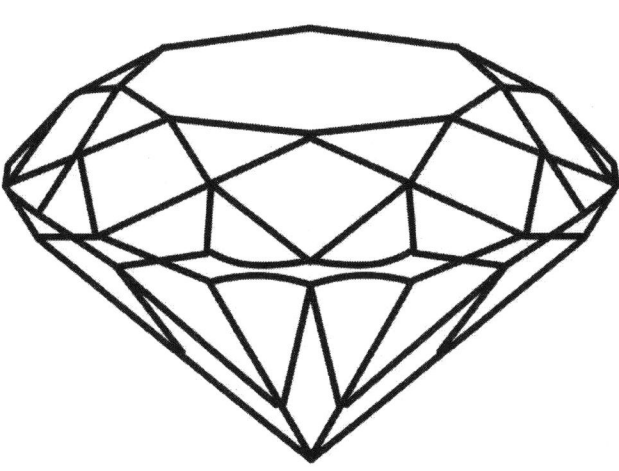

There are __ lines of symmetry.

There are __ lines of symmetry.

There are __ lines of symmetry.

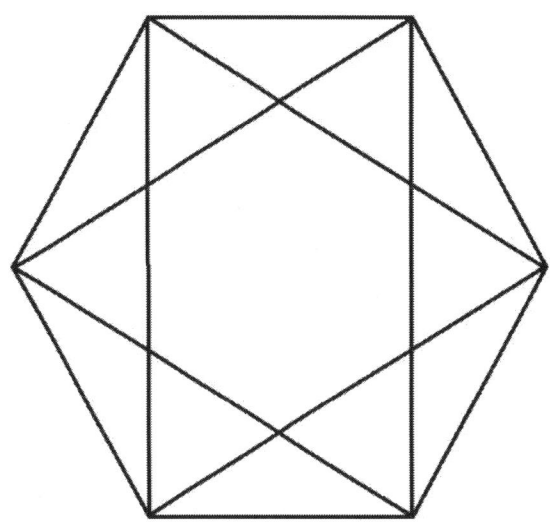

There are __ lines of symmetry.

34 – Making Words

Find the hidden words in these boxes (just like Boggle). Each letter in a word must touch the next (horizontally, vertically, or diagonally).

T	S	N	O
O	A	G	E
T	I	R	L
C	O	S	C

	Z	I	X	
B	S	M	T	J
P	O	S	S	V
W	I	B	L	E
	N	P	R	

R	C	T	A
E	L	G	N
T	R	V	L
H	E	A	O

A	R	Y	P
T	M	R	E
D	I	A	L
T	R	N	G

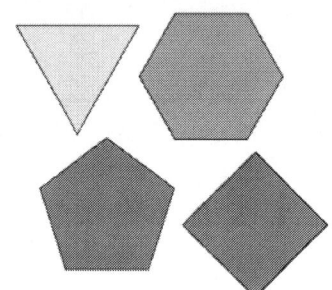

E	X	A	G
H	T	N	O
P	N	U	Q
E	R	A	S

Shapes ⬇

Other words you found ⬇

How many SHAPES did you find?
10-12 Good job.   13 = You rock!!!

How many other words did you find?
15-19 Good job.   20 = You rock!!!

35 – Word Puzzles

Solve these brainteasers

Hints:

Where is a letter or number located in the frame?

What sound does a letter or number make?

Which direction is a word written?

What is missing?

What object is in the frame?

agent

CAUSE (JUST inside CAUSE)

yard (upside down)

BOW BOW BOW / BOW BOW

What do you see?
(common words or phrases we say)

1. _____ 2. _____

3. _____ 4. _____

36 – Identifying Nouns

Directions: **Insert** a noun after each adjective:

round _____	cold _____
sweaty _____	bouncy _____
bendable _____	flying _____
sharp _____	pretty _____
confused _____	soft _____
smooth _____	fast _____
quick _____	hollow _____

37 – What doesn't belong?

1 One shape does NOT belong: It tends to run away from the others. Label it "Catch Me."

2 Another shape does NOT belong: It is too old to play games with the youngsters. Label it "Egypt."

3 This shape does NOT belong: It isn't sure where it it going. Label it "NESW."

4 A shape does NOT belong: It stops too much. Label it "Red."

5 Another shape does NOT belong: It doesn't add much to the discussion. Label it "Plus Size."

38 – Birds in the Air

Find the hidden birds in this Word Search. They are either horizontal, vertical, diagonal, forwards, or backwards.

Unscramble these words.

↓

egipno
binor
cobgimnkird
rotsk
low
udkc
gelsula
dood
arptor
navre

T	D	D	G	O	L	D	E	N	E	Y	E	Q	Q
U	U	U	R	E	D	H	E	A	D	D	Q	Q	P
F	C	C	D	U	C	K	Q	Q	O	Q	Q	Q	I
T	K	K	C	U	D	G	A	D	W	E	L	L	G
E	D	C	W	I	G	E	O	N	D	U	C	K	E
D	U	U	Q	N	S	H	O	V	E	L	E	R	O
Q	C	D	I	Q	R	O	T	P	A	R	Q	Q	N
Q	K	B	L	A	C	K	S	C	O	T	E	R	Q
M	O	T	T	L	E	D	U	C	K	L	A	E	T
R	D	W	H	I	S	T	L	I	N	G	Q	D	L
Q	U	Q	L	Q	N	S	T	O	R	K	Q	I	L
W	C	Q	M	E	R	G	A	N	S	E	R	E	U
O	K	Q	V	M	U	S	C	O	V	Y	Q	G	G
O	Q	A	R	U	D	D	Y	D	U	C	K	N	A
D	R	I	B	G	N	I	K	C	O	Q	Q	I	E
Q	Q	K	C	A	B	S	A	V	N	A	C	K	S
M	A	L	L	A	R	D	L	I	A	T	N	I	P

_____ _____ _____
_____ _____ _____
_____ _____ _____
_____

Bonus: How many types of ducks can you find? _____

39 – The Discovery

While playing alone, a young boy discovers something weird near his village. What do they say to each other?

40 – Where does dirt come from?

41 – Tic-Tac-Toe Writing

1st **Play** Tic-Tac-Toe with a friend until you win. You go first.

2nd **Pick** three characters based on the X's in the game that you won (above).

3rd **Write** a story with those three characters.

42 – What Time is it?

What time is it?

telling time to the nearest minute

___ : ___   ___ : ___   ___ : ___   ___ : ___

___ : ___   ___ : ___   ___ : ___   ___ : ___

Challenge Question: How much time has elapsed from the earliest clock to the latest clock?

Earliest clock __:__   Latest clock __:__   Elapsed time __:__

43 – Where do the circles go?

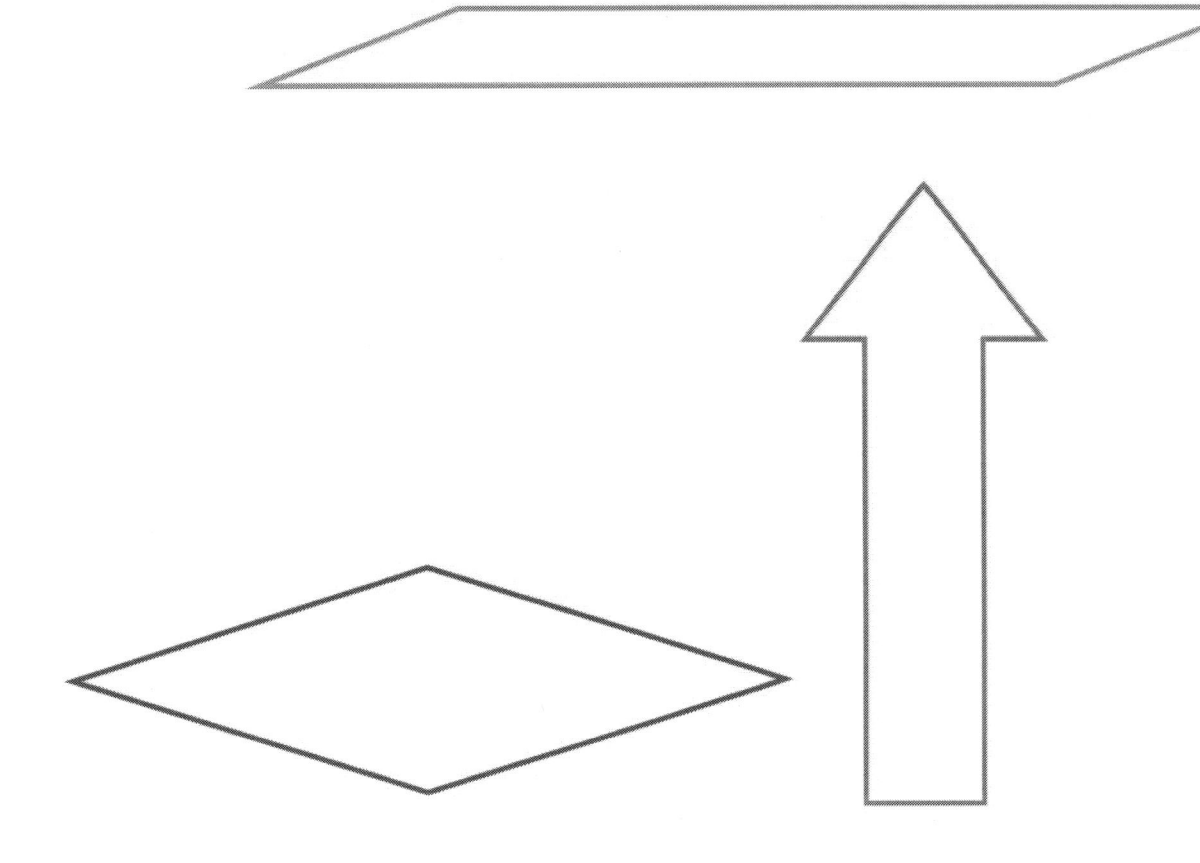

Draw two **circles** inside the <u>arrow</u>.
Draw three **circles** inside the <u>parallelogram</u>.
Draw four **circles** inside the <u>rhombus</u>.
Draw five **circles** overlapping the <u>parallelogram</u>.
Draw six **circles** NOT inside any shape.

44 – All About Me

My favorite color is _____.

My favorite food is _____.

I think with my _____.

I write with my _____ **hand.**

I love _____.

I kick with my _____ foot.

My favorite wild animal is a _____.

My favorite chips are _____.

My favorite bug is _____.

My best friend is _____.

My favorite singer is _____.

My favorite cartoon character is _____.

MY FAVORITE CANDY IS _____.

My favorite drink is _____.

My favorite movie is _____.

I hate to _____.

My favorite pet is a _____.

When I grow up, I want to be a _____.

45 – Where do rocks come from?

46 – Syllables

Directions: Use arrows to connect the syllables of these **Butterfly**-words

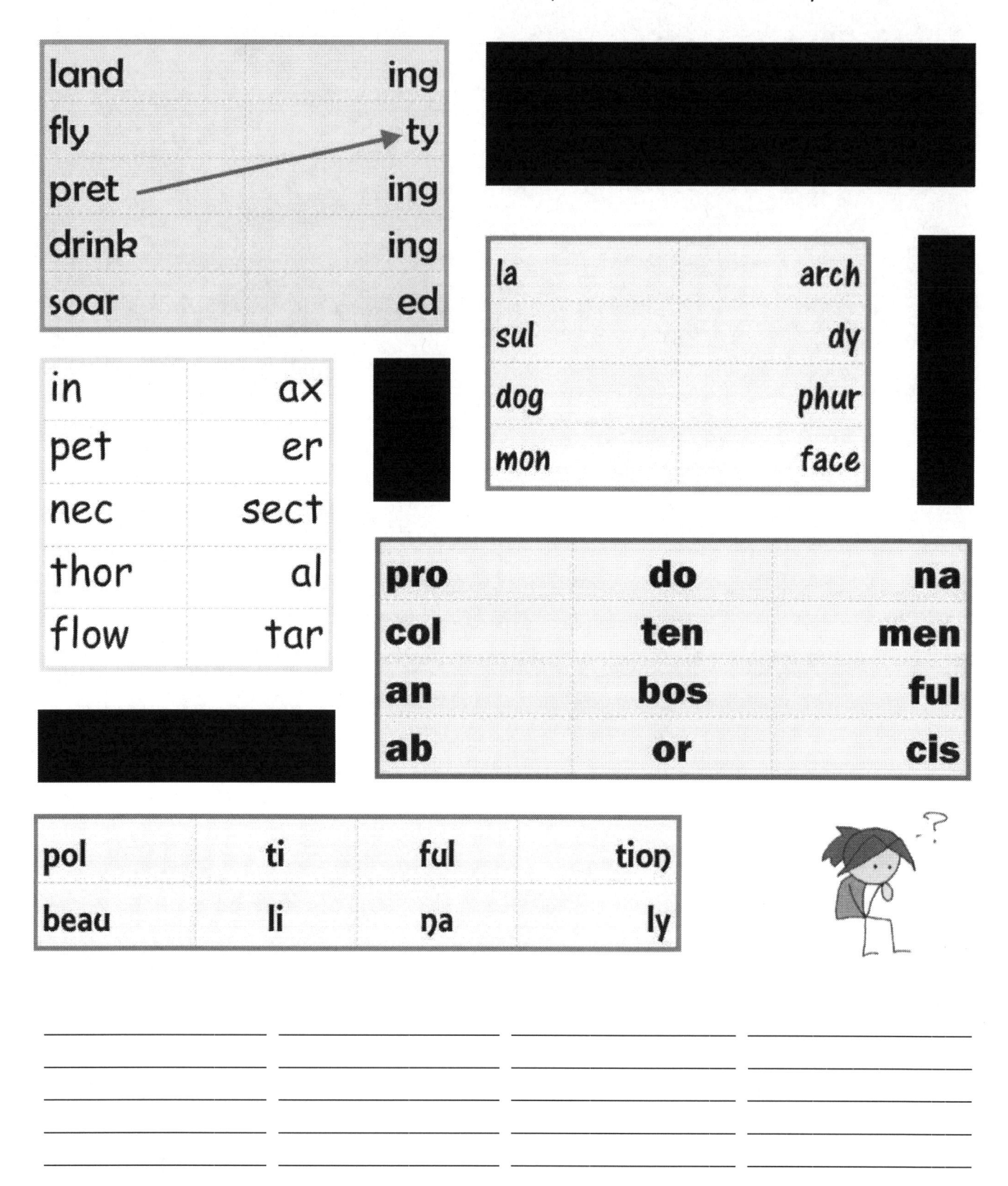

land			ing
fly			ty
pret			ing
drink			ing
soar			ed

la		arch
sul		dy
dog		phur
mon		face

in	ax
pet	er
nec	sect
thor	al
flow	tar

pro	do	na
col	ten	men
an	bos	ful
ab	or	cis

pol	ti	ful	tion
beau	li	na	ly

_____ _____ _____ _____
_____ _____ _____ _____
_____ _____ _____ _____
_____ _____ _____ _____

47 – Context Clues

| The flietr jumped from the lily pad into the water. |

What kind of an animal is a flietr? _____
What clues in the sentence helped you figure this out?
- ✓ _____
- ✓ _____

| The wiglr slithered through the grass on its belly in search of a mouse. |

What kind of an animal is a wiglr? _____
What clues in the sentence helped you figure this out?
- ✓ _____
- ✓ _____

| The sloruner pulled its toes and tail inside its shell to protect it from the hungry predator. |

What kind of an animal is a sloruner? _____
What clues in the sentence helped you figure this out?
- ✓ _____
- ✓ _____

| The aleswam swam through the swamp, swishing its long tail back and forth. |

What kind of an animal is a aleswam? _____
What clues in the sentence helped you figure this out?
- ✓ _____
- ✓ _____

48 – Making Words

Find the hidden words in these boxes (just like Boggle). Each letter in a word must touch the next (horizontally, vertically, or diagonally).

D	E	A	W
R	E	L	H
A	B	S	K
T	R	O	H

	Z	I	X	
B	S	M	T	J
P	O	S	S	V
W	I	B	L	E
	N	P	R	

E	S	U	F
M	O	G	Y
D	O	X	E
M	F	N	K

E	K	W	O
S	A	C	B
N	T	P	E
A	H	E	L

I	N	E	P
N	U	G	H
L	M	N	I
E	I	K	P

Animals ⬇

How many ANIMALS did you find?
19-23 Good job.   **24** = You rock!!!

Other words you found ⬇

How many other words did you find?
15-19 Good job.   **20** = You rock!!!

49 – How does a bud know when to open?

50 – Find the ERRORS

	1	2	3	4	5	6	7	8	9	10
1	1	2	4	4	5	6	7	8	9	10
2	2	4	6	8	6	12	14	16	18	20
3	3	6	9	12	15	18	21	24	27	30
4	4	8	12	14	20	24	26	32	36	40
5	5	10	15	20	25	30	35	40	45	50
6	6	10	18	24	30	35	42	48	56	60
7	7	14	21	28	36	42	49	56	63	70
8	6	16	24	32	40	48	56	64	72	60
9	9	21	27	36	45	54	63	72	81	90
10	10	20	30	40	50	60	70	80	90	100

Circle the 10 errors in the times tables chart above.

Write the correct multiplication sentences below:

Error #1	__ x __ = ____	Error #6	__ x __ = ____
Error #2	__ x __ = ____	Error #7	__ x __ = ____
Error #3	__ x __ = ____	Error #8	__ x __ = ____
Error #4	__ x __ = ____	Error #9	__ x __ = ____
Error #5	__ x __ = ____	Error #10	__ x __ = ____

51 – Word Pairs

Some word pairs ALWAYS go in the same order, like "bacon and eggs." No one says, "I'd like some eggs and bacon." No one! Your job is to find the pairs and write them in the proper order below.

Here are the words you can use (mark them off as you use them below):

Adam, alive, back, bacon, bed, bees, birds, black, breakfast, bride, cause, center, chips, coat, coffee, cream, crime, cup, dead, death, doughnuts, dry, effect, eggs, eggs, Eve, fish, fork, forth, front, fun, games, gentlemen, groom, ham, hammer, high, husband, in, Jack, Jill, key, knife, ladies, law, life, lock, nail, order, out, pepper, punishment, salt, saucer, sugar, tie, white, wife

Write the word pairs below:

_____ and _____   _____ and _____   _____ and _____

_____ and _____   _____ and _____   _____ and _____

_____ and _____   _____ and _____   _____ and _____

_____ and _____   _____ and _____   _____ and _____

_____ and _____   _____ and _____   _____ and _____

_____ and _____   _____ and _____

_____ and _____   _____ and _____   _____ or _____

_____ and _____   _____ and _____   _____ or _____

_____ and _____   _____ and _____   _____ or _____

_____ and _____   _____ and _____   _____ or _____

52 – Multiplication

Solve these multiplication problems and *write* the word name for each product

```
  5 6        4 8        9 3
×   7      ×   8      ×   2
-----      -----      -----
```
→ _____
→ _____
→ _____

```
  5 1        7 4        4 2
×   4      ×   3      ×   9
-----      -----      -----
```
→ _____
→ _____
→ _____

```
  3 3        3 7        9 3
×   6      ×   8      ×   5
-----      -----      -----
```
→ _____
→ _____
→ _____

53 – Cars and Trucks

How many vehicles are ready for the race? __
How many wheels are on these vehicles (count the ones you can't see too)? __
How many drivers do you see? __

How many numbers are odd? __
How many numbers are even? __
How many numbers have a loop? __
How many numbers have a curve? __

54 – How does CAMOUFLAGE keep animals safe?

55 – Word Puzzles

Solve these brainteasers

Hints:

Where is a letter or number located in the frame?

What sound does a letter or number make?

Which direction is a word written?

What is missing?

What object is in the frame?

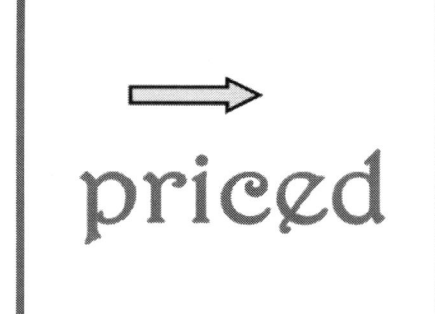

N⊙	M8
→ priced	lookUleap

What do you see?
(common words or phrases we say)

1. _____   2. _____

3. _____   4. _____

56 – Rectangles

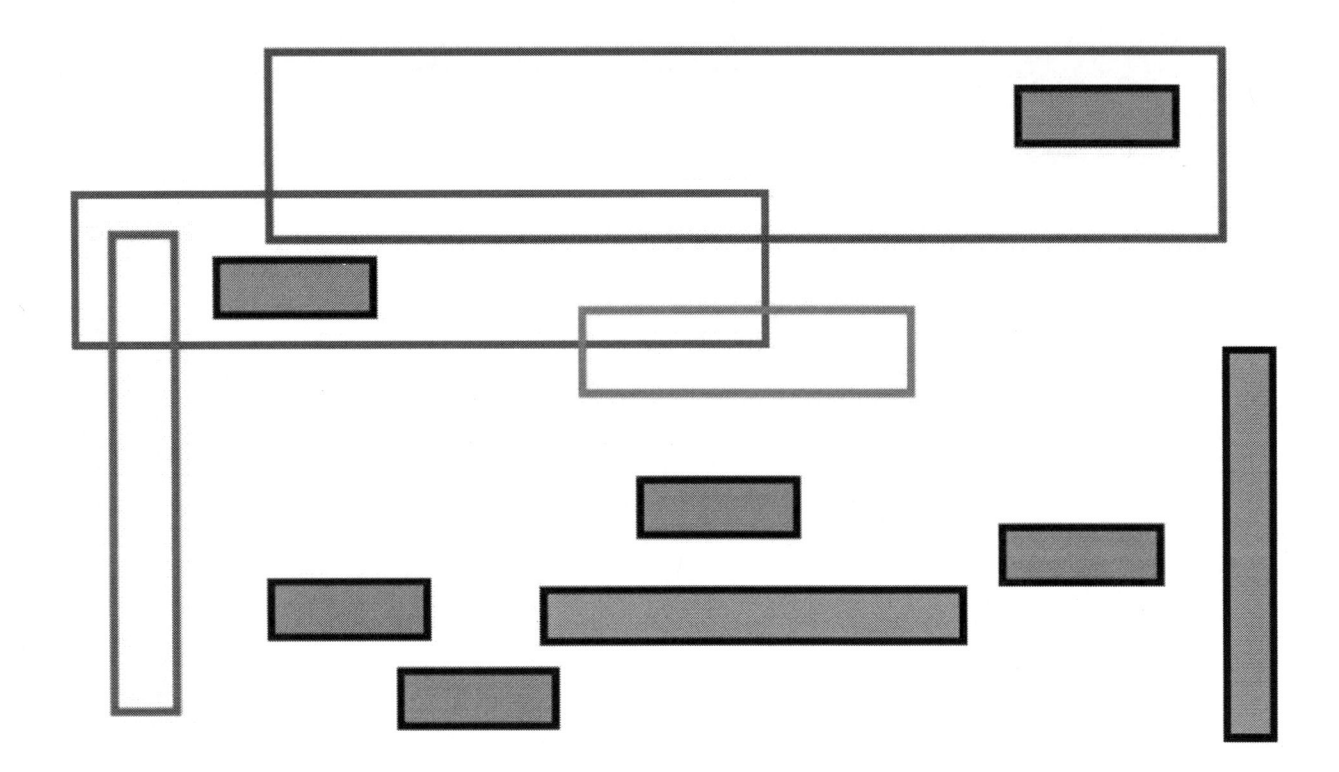

How many **shaded** rectangles do you see? ___

How rectangles **touch** the edge of another rectangle? ___

How many rectangles are **alone** (not in another rectangle or touching any edge)? ___

How many **total** rectangles are there? ___

57 – Making Words

Find the hidden words in these boxes (just like Boggle). Each letter in a word must touch the next (horizontally, vertically, or diagonally).

L	T	W	G
E	F	R	I
E	A	B	U
T	R	K	N

	Z	I	X	
B	S	M	T	J
P	O	S	S	V
W	I	B	L	E
	N	P	R	

N	R	N	E
C	A	B	I
H	U	M	V
B	S	S	O

R	O	T	S
P	O	W	R
E	D	L	E
T	A	E	F

D	D	A	G
T	S	E	R
E	D	S	B
M	E	A	L

Plant nouns ⬇

Other words you found ⬇

How many PLANT nouns did you find?
13-16 Good job.   **17** = You rock!!!

How many other words did you find?
15-19 Good job.   **20** = You rock!!!

58 – Which things are yellow?

59 – Kid Fractions

How many TOTAL kids are there? _____

What fraction of the kids are making a SPLASH? _____
What fraction of the kids are HOLDING something? _____
What fraction of the kids are STANDING? _____
What fraction of the kids wear something on their HEAD? _____

What fraction of the kids wear something on their FEET? _____

What fraction of the kids are in the AIR? _____
What fraction of the kids are under WATER? _____

60 – Word Name (thousands)

Write word name for each five-digit number

standard form　　　　　　　　　　　**word name**

37,517 → _____

94,813 → _____

60,121 → _____

73,317 → _____

51,018 → _____

85,514 → _____

56,521 → _____

48,130 → _____

79,215 → _____

38,781 → _____

67,852 → _____

51,103 → _____

30,671 → _____

93,781 → _____

76,517 → _____

89,190 → _____

61 – Anagrams Challenge

Directions: Match the pair of anagrams (use a connecting arrow).

Directions: Write the anagram pairs below:

_____ and _____   _____ and _____   _____ and _____
_____ and _____   _____ and _____   _____ and _____
_____ and _____   _____ and _____

62 – Different is okay...

Describe four ways that you are <u>different</u> from a friend in what you do for fun.

1

2

3

4

63 – How does an insect find a flower?

64 – Triangles

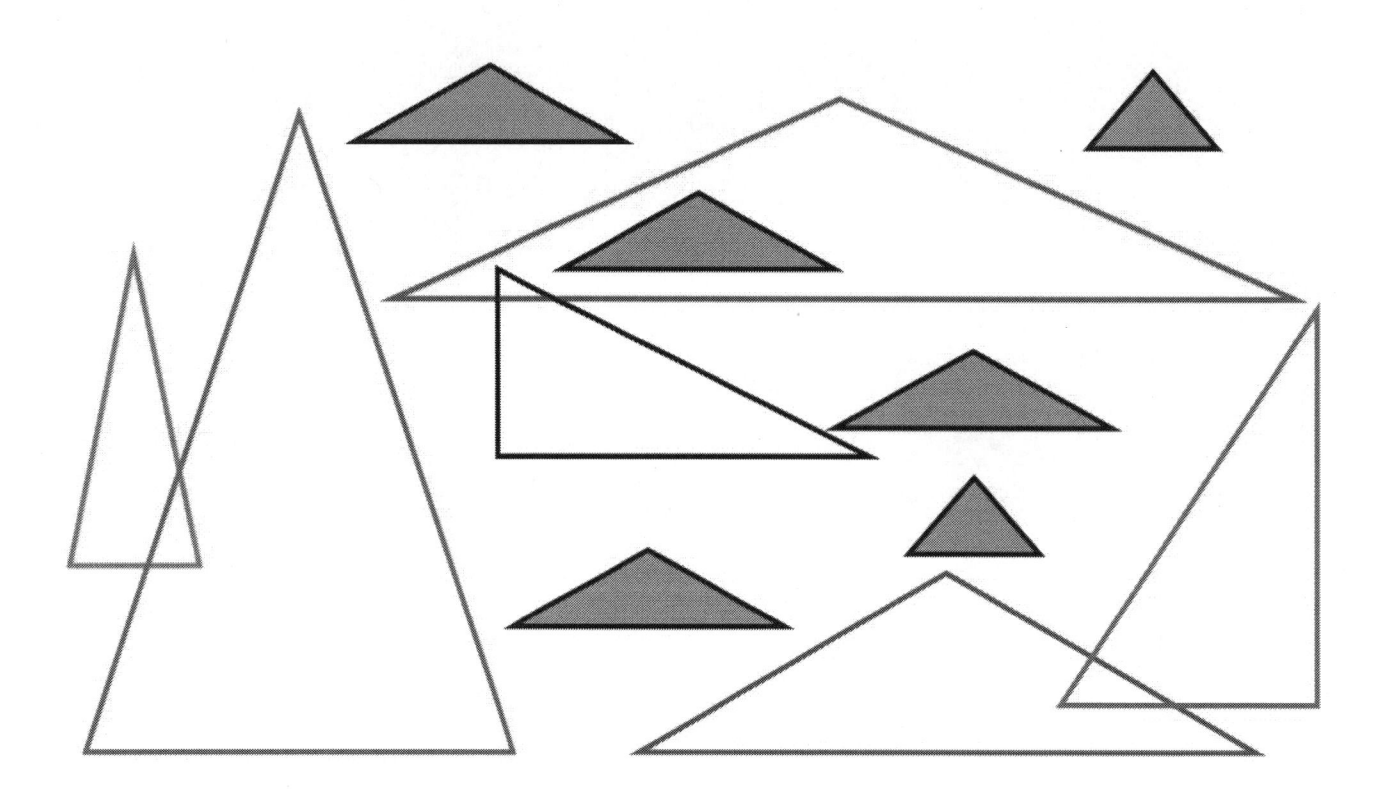

How many **shaded** triangles do you see? ___

How triangles **touch** the edge of another triangle? ___

How many triangles are **alone** (not in another triangle or touching any edge)? ___

How many **total** triangles are there? ___

65 – Looking into the past

What is the **SAME** and what is **DIFFERENT**?

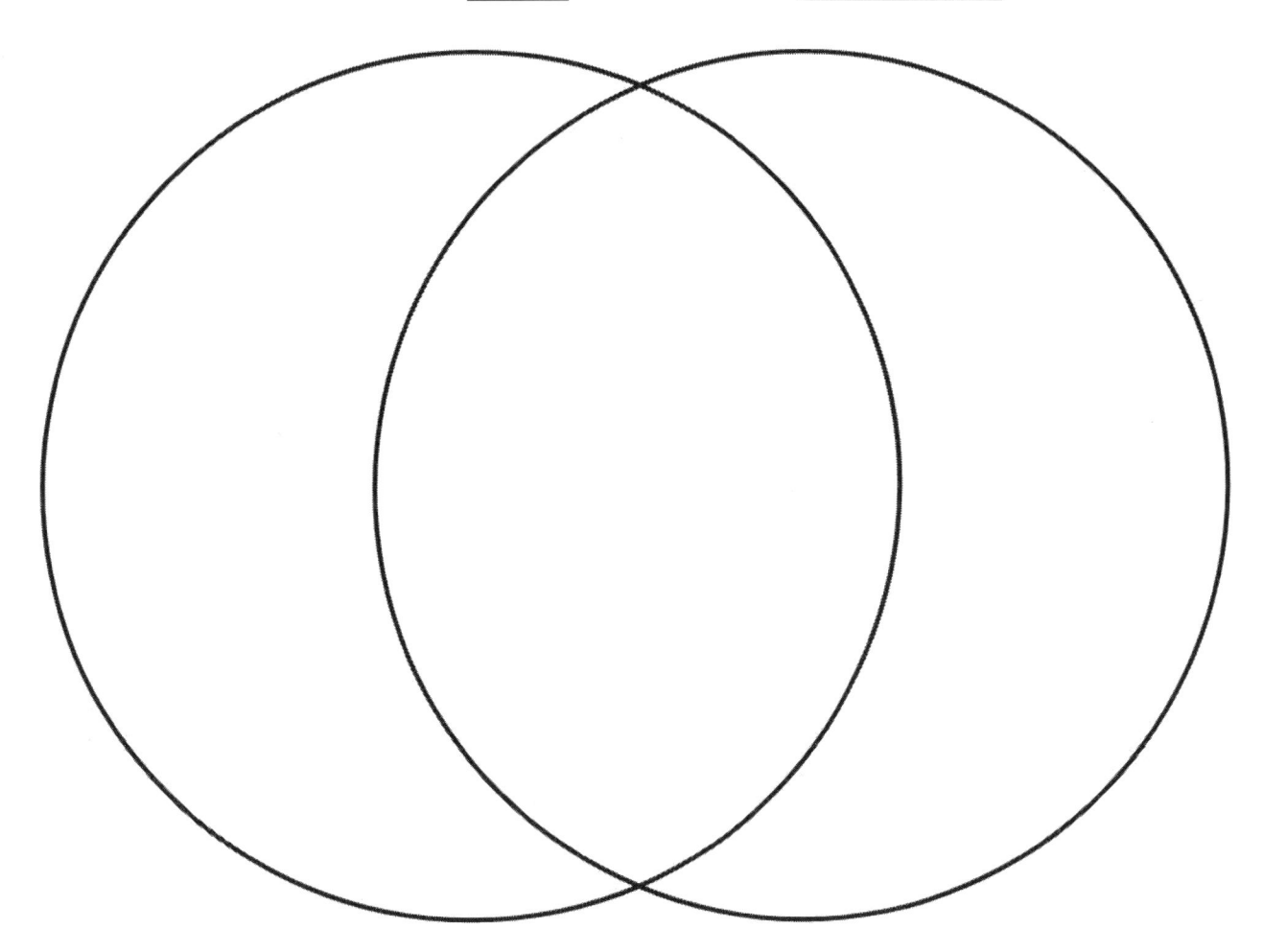

66 – Spiders Are My Friend

charaind
nopuce
repacte
gnafs
tolm
ebw
thige
unth
noevm
kils

Do you like spiders or are you afraid of them? _____
Why? _____
Would you like to have one as a pet? _____
_____
_____

67 – Use Your Imagination

As a boy is fishing in a pond, he turns to find a monster right behind him. What do they say to each other?

68 – Word Puzzles

Solve these brainteasers

Hints:

Where is a letter or number located in the frame?

What sound does a letter or number make?

Which direction is a word written?

What is missing?

What object is in the frame?

4cast	T E Stomach
tis + RELAX	man board

What DO YOU see?
(common words or phrases we say)

1. _____   2. _____

3. _____   4. _____

69 – Weather Sudoku

Use <u>reasoning</u> and <u>logic</u> to fill in each 4×4 grid so that each ROW, COLUMN and SQUARE has all four weather symbols.

summer   fall   winter   spring

70 – What can you see when hiking?

71 – Synonyms for the letter B

Directions: Match the pairs of synonyms with the scrambled words on the right. The first is done for you.

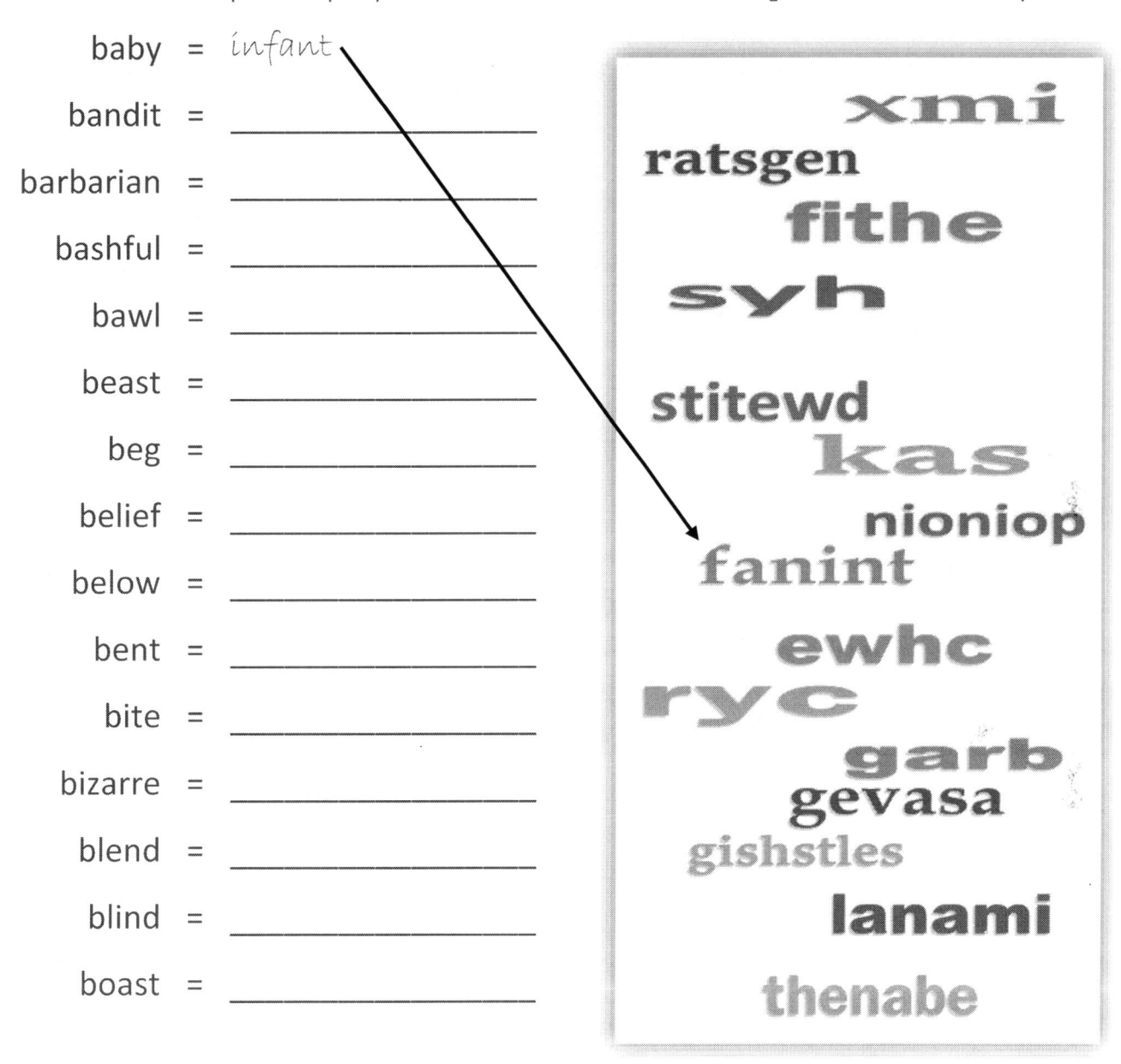

baby = *infant*

bandit = _____

barbarian = _____

bashful = _____

bawl = _____

beast = _____

beg = _____

belief = _____

below = _____

bent = _____

bite = _____

bizarre = _____

blend = _____

blind = _____

boast = _____

xmi
ratsgen
fithe
syh
stitewd
kas
nioniop
fanint
ewhc
ryc
garb
gevasa
gishstles
lanami
thenabe

Directions: Write sentences using A-synonyms, placing two different words in each sentence.

1

2

3

72 – Counting and Comparing Coins

How many **dimes** are there? ___
How many **quarters** are there? ___
How many **pennies** are there? ___
How many more **quarters** are there than **dollars**? ___ - ___ = ___
How many more **pennies** are there than **nickels**? ___ - ___ = ___
How many more **pennies** are there than **dimes**? ___ - ___ = ___
What is the *value* of the **dimes**? $_____
What is the *value* of the **quarters**? $_____
What is the *value* of the **pennies**? $_____
What is the *value* of the **dollars**? $_____
Compare the *value* of the **pennies** to the **dimes**: $_____ > $_____
Compare the *value* of the **quarters** to the **dimes**: $_____ < $_____
What is the *value* of the **nickels** and **dimes**? $_____ + $_____ = $_____
What is the *value* of the **dollars** and **pennies**? $_____ + $_____ = $_____
What is the total *value* of ALL the coins? $_____

73 – Is it okay to kill bugs?

74 – Steps

it is cooling as the evening approaches

a rabbit hops down the stairs

a cloud blocks the sun for a moment

a beetle lands on the railing

a squirrel chatters in a tree

a snake slithers in the bushes

a honeybee flies in pursuit of nectar

a hiker approaches from a nearby trail

a caterpillar makes its way across a stair

A LEAF FALLS TO THE GROUND

75 – Spelling Unscramble for Our Earth

Directions: Unscramble the letters to form words related to Earth Day (the picture may give you a clue).

pirtofont = _____

noveirtnmen = _____

mdpu = _____

ipna = _____

raspy = _____

rete = _____

refowl = _____

pomcots = _____

76 – Do you like to be alone?

77 – Sums and Differences

456 714 94 284
540
873 400 700 949
689 181 589 728
629 479 751
97

How many numbers are <u>ODD</u>? _____

How many numbers are <u>EVEN</u>? _____

What is the sum of the numbers with a <u>nine</u>? _____

What is the sum of the numbers with a <u>five</u>? _____

What is the sum of the numbers in their <u>five hundreds</u>? _____

What is the difference between the <u>largest</u> ODD number and the <u>smallest</u> EVEN number? _____ - _____ = _____

What is the difference between the <u>largest</u> EVEN number and the <u>smallest</u> ODD number? _____ - _____ = _____

78 – What can you buy with a DOLLAR?

Greece

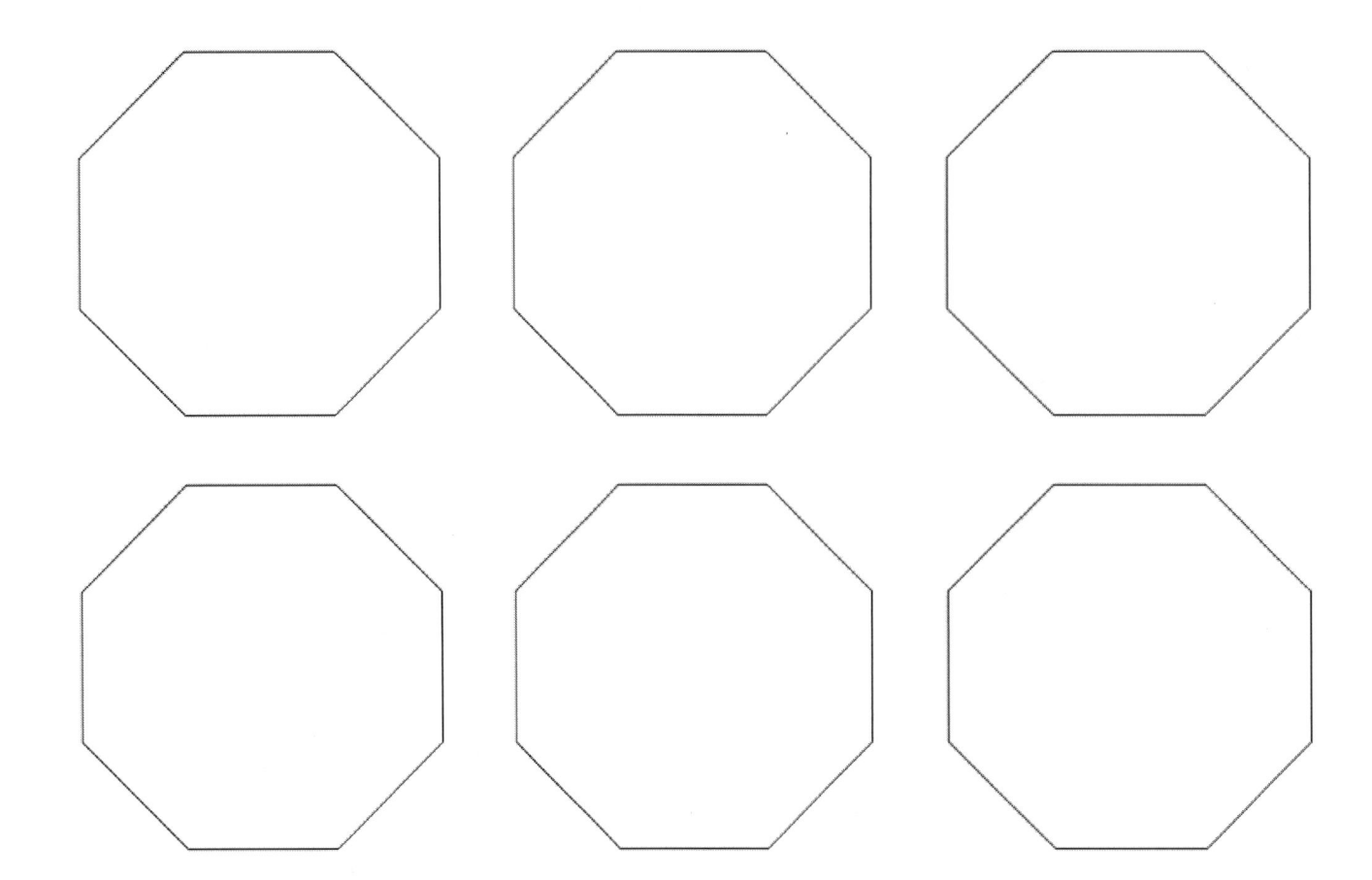

79 – How do cracks form in the Earth?

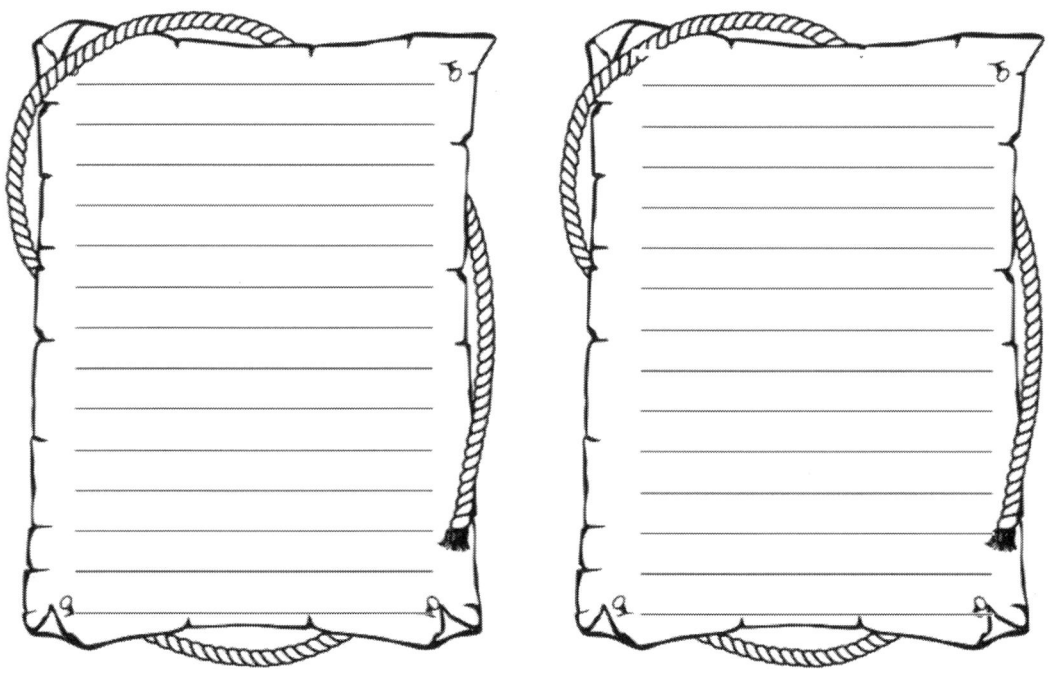

80 – Dracula and the Scared Pumpkin

Dracula walks up to a pumpkin in the middle of the night. He brings his foot back to give it a hard kick when he hears a voice. What do they say to each other?

81 – Sudoku and the Human Body

Use <u>reasoning</u> and <u>logic</u> to fill in each 4×4 grid so that the numbers 1, 2, 3 and 4 are in each **row**, **column** and **square**.

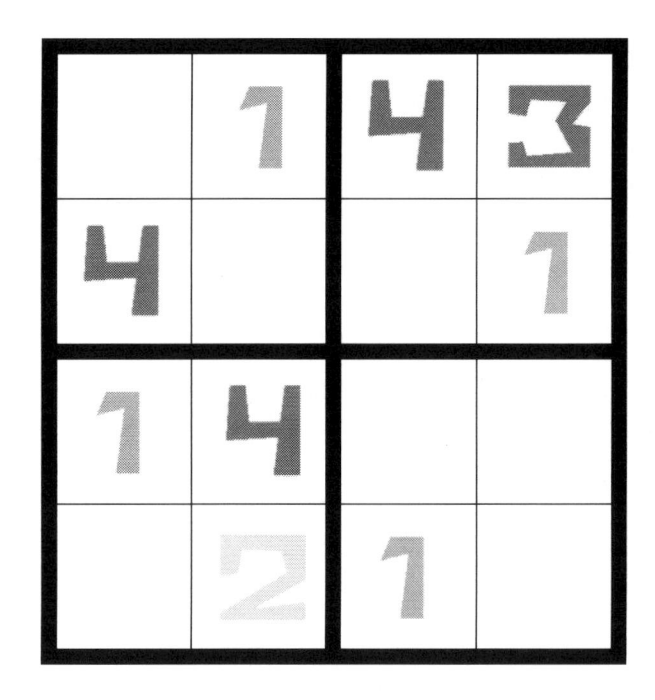

1-2-3-4

	1	4	3
4			1
1		4	
	2	1	

Did you know that the heart pumps about 22 cups of blood into your lungs and out to the rest of your body every minute?

Did you know that food is mostly made of water, protein, carbohydrates and fat?

Did you know that many things your body does you can't control, like when your pupils dilate to let in more light in a dark room? You can't tell you pupils to get bigger. It just happens.

2	1		3
		2	
		1	2
1			4

82 – Why do we cry?

83 – Identifying Nouns

Directions: **Insert** a noun after each adjective:

beating _____	fast _____
spinning _____	flying _____
cute _____	straight _____
tall _____	closed _____
smiling _____	flowery _____
struggling _____	long _____
open _____	scared _____

84 – What doesn't belong?

① One triangle does NOT belong: It gets eaten by hungry mice when left on the table. Label it "**Yellow**."

② Another triangle does NOT belong: It sees everything and reminds you about your mistakes too often. Label it "**Gotcha**."

③ A triangle does NOT belong: It is very attractive, too attractive, and keeps getting attached to stuff. Label it "**Clinger**."

④ Another triangle does NOT belong: It is rather goofy and says silly things at the wrong time. Label it "**Sorry**."

⑤ This triangle does NOT belong: It gets confused about its own shape. Label it "**Shapy**."

85 – Why do ducks float in the water?

86 – Tic-Tac-Toe Writing

1st **Play** Tic-Tac-Toe with a friend until you win.

2nd **Pick** three characters based on the X's in the game that you won (above).

3rd **Write** a story with those three characters.

87 – Analyzing What People Say

"Nobody can hurt me without my permission."

- Mahatma Gandhi

My Thoughts and Opinions

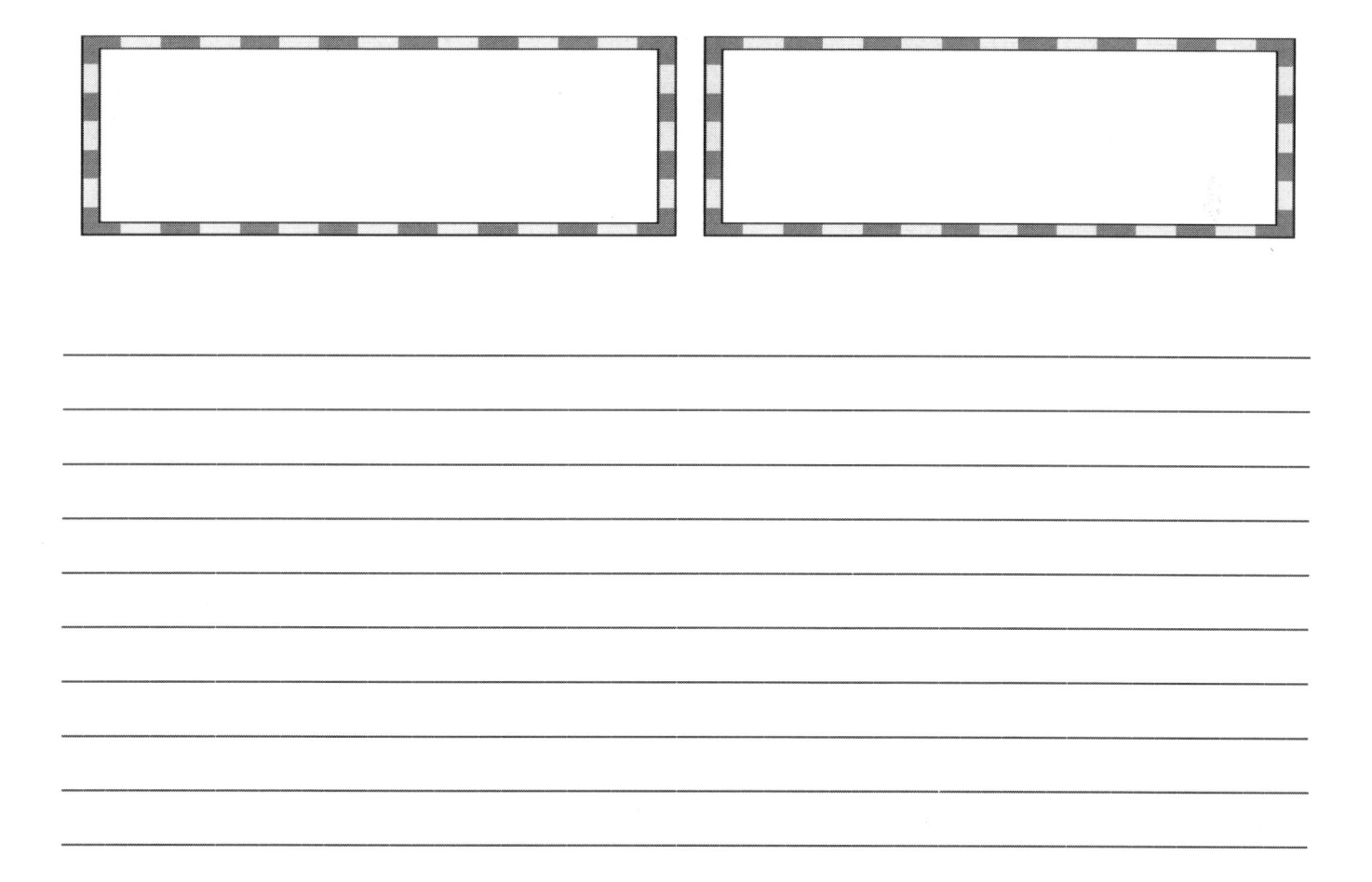

_____
_____
_____
_____
_____
_____
_____
_____
_____
_____

88 – What does the word "old" mean?

89 – What is MATH all about?

Sao Tome and Principe

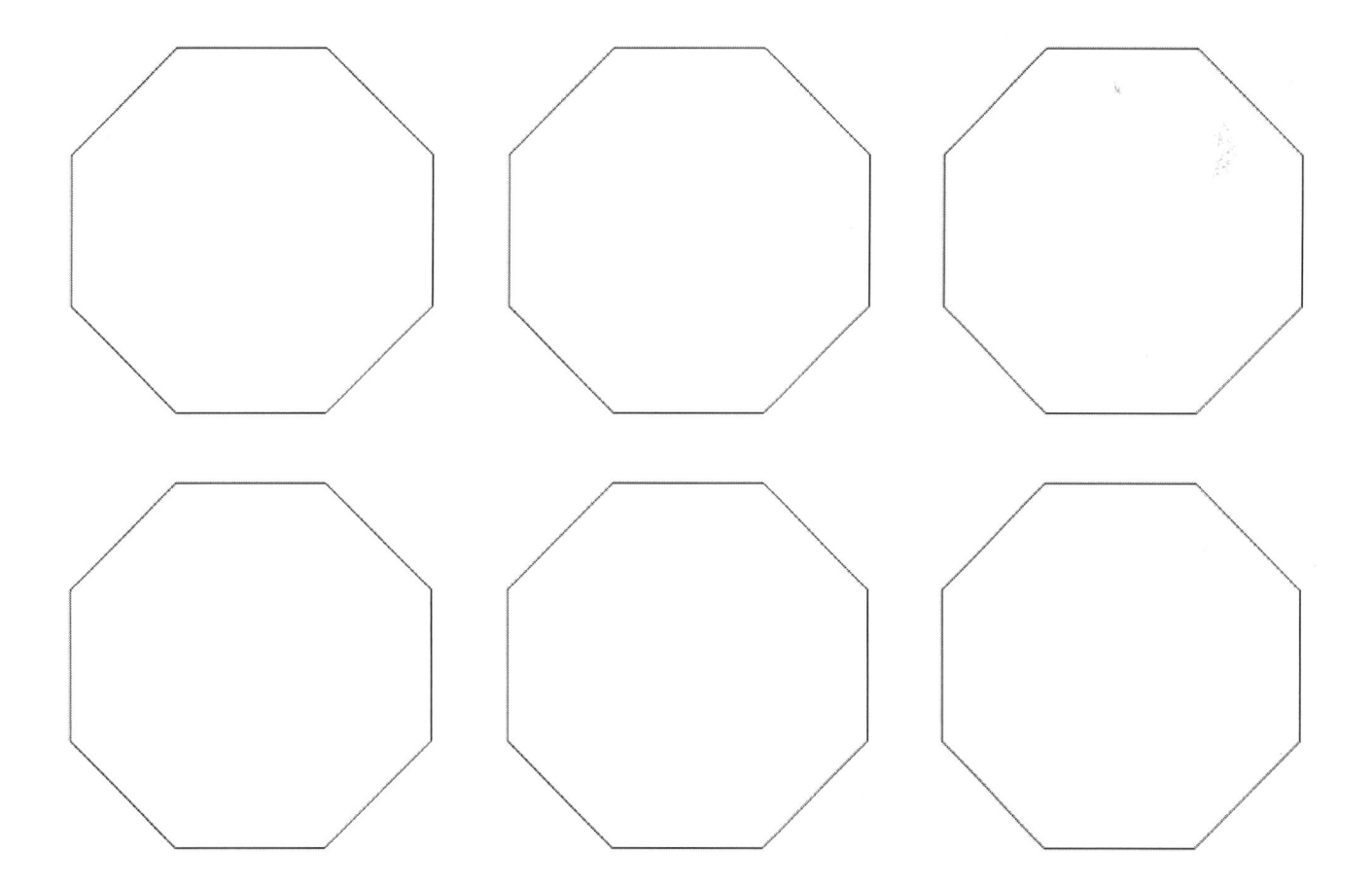

90 – What Time is it?

What time is it?

telling time to the nearest minute

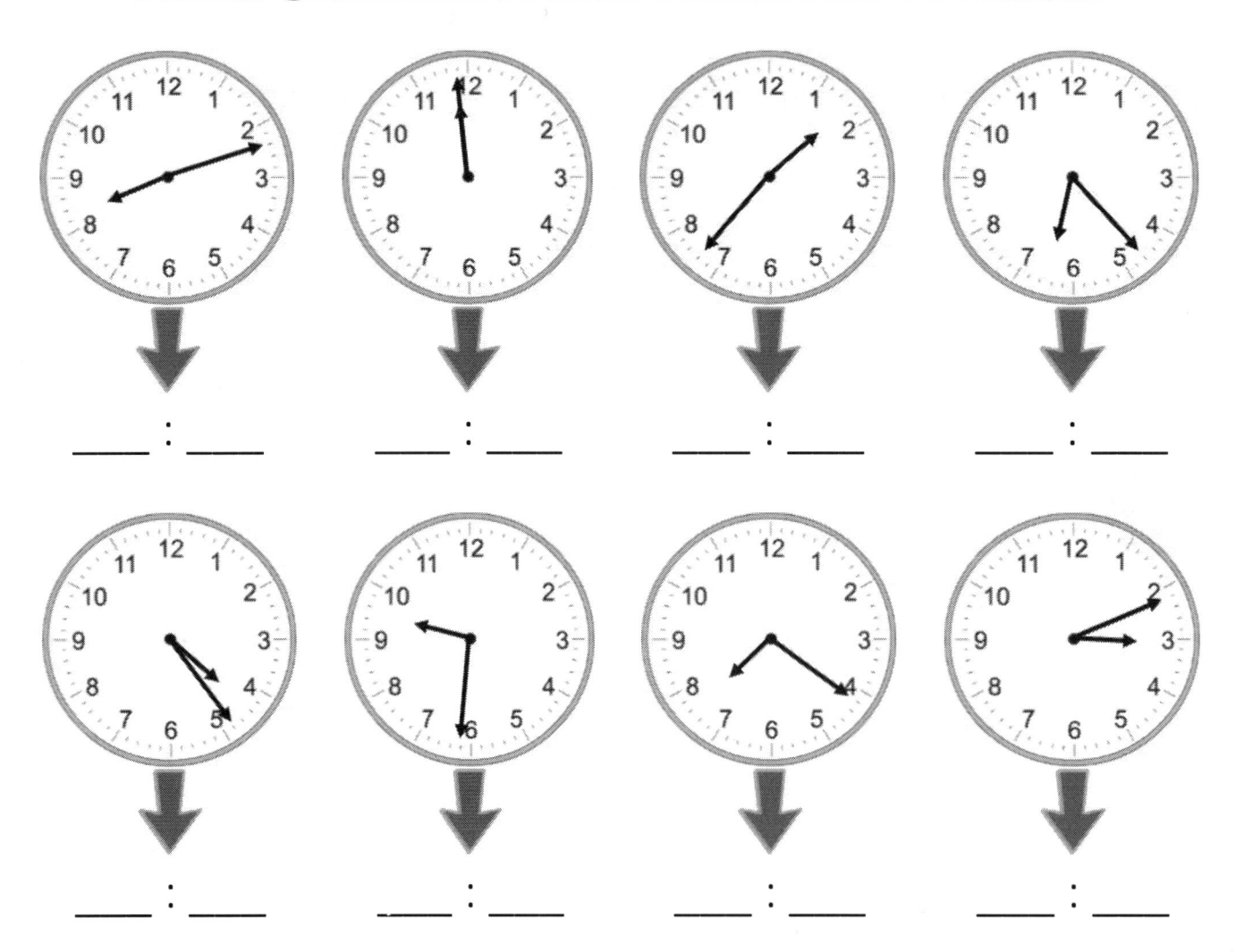

___ : ___   ___ : ___   ___ : ___   ___ : ___

___ : ___   ___ : ___   ___ : ___   ___ : ___

Challenge Question: How much time has elapsed from the earliest clock to the latest clock?

Earliest clock __:__   Latest clock __:__   Elapsed time __:__

91 – What is the job of your brain?

92 – Syllables

Directions: Use arrows to connect the syllables of these **Spider**-words.

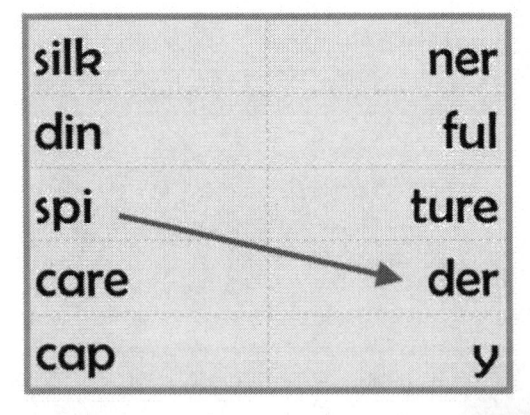

silk	ner
din	ful
spi	ture
care	der
cap	y

pred	a	pod
ar	om	tor
ven	a	cle
spir	thro	ous

molt	line
egg	y
drag	male
stick	ing
fe	sac

spi	ner	nid
a	der	men
cam	rach	ette
ab	ou	ling
spin	do	flage

in	i	te	brate
hes	ver	ta	tion

_____ _____ _____ _____
_____ _____ _____ _____
_____ _____ _____ _____
_____ _____ _____ _____
_____ _____ _____ _____
                        _____

93 – What is on the inside of you?

94 – Find the ERRORS

	1	2	3	4	5	6	7	8	9	10
1	1	2	3	4	5	6	7	8	9	10
2	2	4	6	8	10	12	14	16	14	20
3	3	6	9	10	15	18	21	24	27	30
4	4	6	12	16	20	22	28	32	36	20
5	5	10	15	20	25	30	35	50	45	50
6	6	12	18	24	30	35	42	48	54	60
7	7	16	21	28	35	42	49	56	63	70
8	8	16	24	30	40	48	56	64	72	80
9	9	20	27	36	45	54	63	54	81	90
10	10	20	30	40	50	60	70	80	90	100

Circle the 10 errors in the times tables chart above.

Write the correct multiplication sentences below:

Error #1 __ x __ = ____   Error #6 __ x __ = ____
Error #2 __ x __ = ____   Error #7 __ x __ = ____
Error #3 __ x __ = ____   Error #8 __ x __ = ____
Error #4 __ x __ = ____   Error #9 __ x __ = ____
Error #5 __ x __ = ____   Error #10 __ x __ = ____

95 – Word Pairs

Some word pairs ALWAYS go in the same order, like "salt and pepper." No one says, "Pass me the pepper and salt." No one! Your job is to find the pairs and write them in the proper order below.

Here are the words you can use (mark them off as you use them below):

address, beans, cheese, cream, demand, down, easy, error, fall, found, go, later, lost, man, name, nice, pants, peace, peaches, pen, pencil, pepper, pork, pots, rain, read, right, rise, salt, shine, shirt, shoes, slide, slip, soap, socks, sooner, sour, stars, stripes, suit, supply, sweet, tall, thin, tie, tie, touch, trial, up, war, water, wife, wine, write, wrong,

Write the word pairs below:

_____ and _____   _____ and _____   _____ and _____

_____ and _____   _____ and _____   _____ and _____

_____ and _____   _____ and _____   _____ and _____

_____ and _____   _____ and _____   _____ and _____

_____ and _____   _____ and _____   _____ and _____

_____ and _____   _____ and _____   _____ and _____

_____ and _____   _____ and _____

_____ and _____   _____ and _____

_____ and _____   _____ and _____   _____ or _____

_____ and _____   _____ and _____   _____ or _____

96 – Do plants have SKIN or MUSCLES or BONES?

97 – Word Puzzles

Solve these brainteasers

Hints:
Where is a letter or number located in the frame?

What sound does a letter or number make?

Which direction is a word written?

What is missing?

What object is in the frame?

min between ute	death LIFE
yarPLAYd	THOUGHT an

What do you see?
(common words or phrases we say)

1. _____   2. _____

3. _____   4. _____

98 – Rectangles

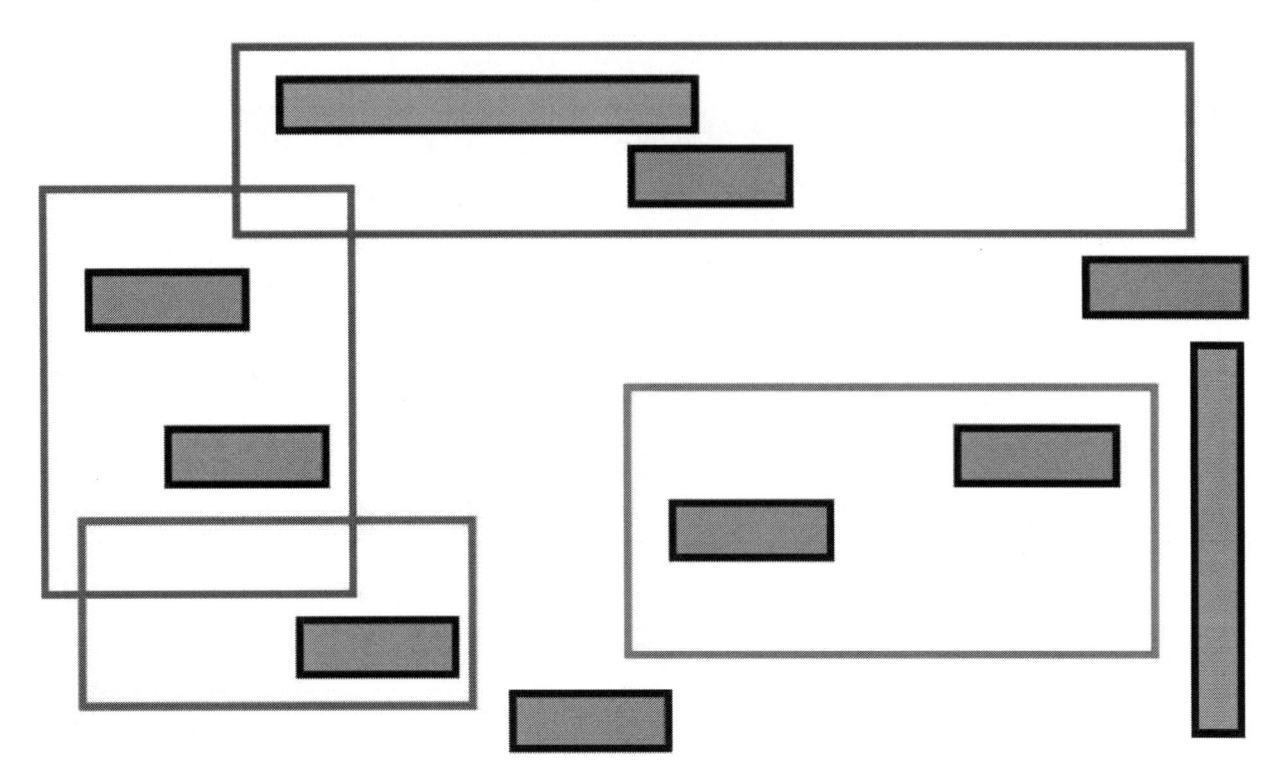

1. How many **shaded** rectangles do you see? ___

2. How rectangles **touch** the edge of another rectangle? ___

3. How many rectangles are **alone** (not in another rectangle or touching any edge)? ___

4. How many **total** rectangles are there? ___

99 – Context Clues

| The girl watched two meowmy licking their paws and swishing their tails. |

What kind of an animal is a meowmy? _____
What clues in the sentence helped you figure this out?
- ✓ _____
- ✓ _____

| Karen waited as the hoarsply stomped its hooves and galloped across the field. |

What kind of an animal is a hoarsply? _____
What clues in the sentence helped you figure this out?
- ✓ _____
- ✓ _____

| She wanted to see if all brazes had black and white stripes and a fluffy black tail. |

What kind of an animal is a braze? _____
What clues in the sentence helped you figure this out?
- ✓ _____
- ✓ _____

| Her brother watched as the wellfits broke the surface of the water and blew water out of its spout. |

What kind of an animal is a wellfit? _____
What clues in the sentence helped you figure this out?
- ✓ _____
- ✓ _____

100 – What tickles your skin?

Answers

to some of the most challenging puzzles in this workbook

Anagrams Challenge (page 2): brag and grab, fired and fried, harps and sharp, lemon and melon, nails and snail, seal and sale, spray and prays, ticks and stick

Making Words – COLORS (page 4): red, blue, green, yellow, brown, white, black, purple, orange, gray, silver, gold, beige, pink, peach

Word Puzzles (page 6): all in good time, elevate, up for grabs, one step forward, two steps back

Synonyms A-answers (page 13): desert, stomach, over, irrational, pain, get, love, foreign, similar, loyalty, permit, entertain, furious, irritate, reply

Spelling Unscramble (page 18): choke, sorting, factory, reflect, think, healthy, frustrating, exercise

Making Words – NUMBERS (page 19): zero, one, two, three, four, five, six, seven, eight, nine, ten, eleven, twelve, thirteen, fourteen

Word Puzzles (page 21): you win some, you lose some, calm before the storm, all for nothing, missing in action

Making Words – SHAPES (page 34): circle, oval, triangle, square, rectangle, pentagon, hexagon, octagon, cube, cone, pyramid, star, heart

Word Puzzles (page 35): double agent, just in case, backyard, elbow

Context Clues (page 47): **1)** frog clues: jumped, lily pad, water; **2)** snake clues: slithered, belly, mouse; **3)** turtle clues: toes and tail, shell ; **4)** alligator clues: swamp, swishing its long tail

Making Words – ANIMALS (page 48): cat, dog, ox, fox, elephant, ant, bee, monkey mule, horse, cow, elk, mouse, moose, deer, penguin, bat, snake, whale, hen, rat, pig, gnu, mink

Word Pairs (page 51): salt and pepper, Adam and Eve, bacon and eggs, back and forth, bed and breakfast, birds and bees, bride and groom, cause and effect, coat and tie, coffee and doughnuts, cream and sugar, crime and punishment, cup and saucer, fish and chips, front and center, fun and games, ham and eggs, hammer and nail, high and dry, husband and wife, Jack and Jill, knife and fork, ladies and gentlemen, law and order, lock and key, life **or** death, dead **or** alive, black **and/or** white, in **and/or** out

Word Puzzles (page 55): entire, mate, overpriced, look before you leap

How Many… (page 56): 8 shaded, 4 touching, 6 alone, 16 total

Making Words – PLANTS (page 57): tree, bush, grass, flower, weed, petal, seed, stem, blade, trunk, bark, leaf, roots, moss, branch, twig, vine

Anagrams Challenge (page 61): stove and votes, spark and parks, meal and male, rinse and siren, soil and oils, paws and wasp, diary and dairy, ocean and canoe

How Many… (page 64): 6 shaded, 6 touching, 4 alone, 15 total

Word Puzzles (page 68): forecast, upset stomach, sit back and relax, man overboard

Synonyms B-answers (page 71): infant, thief, savage, shy, cry, animal, ask, opinion, beneath, twisted, chew, strange, mix, sightless, brag

Spelling Unscramble (page 75): footprint, environment, dump, pain, spray, tree, flower, compost

Word Pairs (page 95): lost and found, man and wife, name and address, nice and easy, peaches and cream, pen and pencil, pork and beans, pots and pants, read and write, right and/or wrong, rise and fall, salt and pepper, shirt and tie, shoes and socks, slip and slide, soap and water, stars and stripes, suit and tie, supply and demand, sweet and sour, tall and thin, touch and go, trial and error, up and down, war and peace, wine and cheese, rain or shine, sooner or later,

Word Puzzles (page 97): be there in a minute, life after death, play in the yard, an afterthought

How Many… (page 98): 10 shaded, 3 touching, 3 alone, 16 total

Context Clues (page 99): **1)** lions clues: paws, tails; **2)** horse clues: hooves, galloped; **3)** zebras clues: black & white stripes, black tail; **4)** whale : broke the surface, spout

Sudoku

page 7

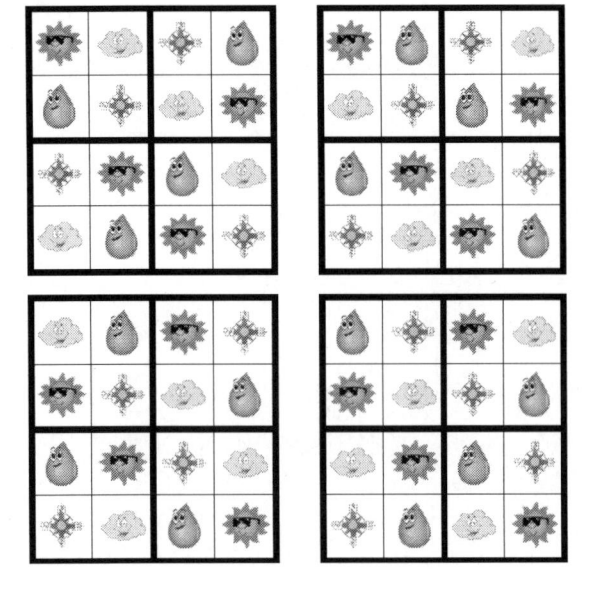

page 32

1	3	2	4
4	2	3	1
2	1	4	3
3	4	1	2

Did you know that the heart is about the size of your fist?

Did you know that people in Bangkok cook and eat fat and juicy grubs?

Did you know that each part of the brain is responsible for the things that you do with your body?

Did you know that you have 206 bones in your body?

1	3	4	2
2	4	3	1
3	2	1	4
4	1	2	3

page 69

page 81

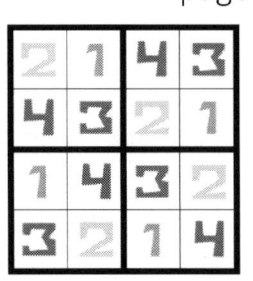

2	1	4	3
4	3	2	1
1	4	3	2
3	2	1	4

Did you know that the heart pumps about 22 cups of blood into your lungs and out to the rest of your body every minute?

Did you know that food is mostly made of water, protein, carbohydrates and fat?

Did you know that many things your body does you can't control, like when your pupils dilate to let in more light in a dark room? You can't tell you pupils to get bigger. It just happens.

2	1	4	3
3	4	2	1
4	3	1	2
1	2	3	4

Made in the USA
Coppell, TX
28 December 2024